Jesus Is Coming

A Different Perspective

Jesus Is Coming—
A Different Perspective

Copyright © 2006 by Ervin Steele

All Rights Reserved

ISBN:1-59352-257-6

Published by:
CSN Books
7287 Birchcreek Road
San Diego, CA 92119
Toll Free: 1-866-757-9953
www.CSNbooks.com

All Scripture quotations, unless otherwise indicated, are taken from the King James Version.

No part of this publication may be reproduced, stored in a retrieval system, or transmitted in any way by any means—electronic, mechanical, photocopy, recording, or otherwise, without the prior permission of the copyright holder, except as provided by USA copyright law.

Printed in the United States of America.

Dedication

I dedicate this book to my precious wife, Gwen of forty-four years and mother of our seven children. She has lovingly supported me through my many years of compiling this manuscript.

Acknowledgments

This book would never have been written, but for the challenges issued by my friend and co-worker, Leonard Cleaver who has gone to be with the Lord. It was Leonard who made me prove the doctrines that I easily accepted in my early Christian life. His challenges have proven invaluable to me in preparing to write this book.

Table of Contents

FOREWORD viii

CHAPTER 1
TWO PREMISES REGARDING THE LORD'S IMMINENT RETURN 9
  Jesus Is Coming: A Different Perspective
  (the Premise Stated) 9
    Where the Church is Today 9
    The Seven Feasts of the Lord 11
    Pentecost and Wave-Loaves Offering 15
    The Feast of Trumpets 17
    The Day of Atonement 20
    How the 70th Week Ends 21
    The Feast of Tabernacles 22
    In the Fullness of Time (the Premise Restated) . 23
    The Servant 23

CHAPTER 2
  WATCHFULNESS IN VIEW OF THE RETURN OF OUR LORD 29
  Events That Must Occur Before the
  Resurrection 30
  Probable Events That Will Occur Before the
  Resurrection 34
  An Event That Will Occur Before the
  Resurrection 37
    The Commission 37
    The Commission Given: Revelation 10 38
    The Day of Vengeance 41

CHAPTER 3
EVENTS OF THE 70TH WEEK 45
The First Half of the 70th Week 46
- The Trumpets 47
- The Bowls of Wrath 53
- The Two Witnesses 56
The Resurrection-Wrath Day 64

CHAPTER 4
THE END TIMES 69
Resources for the Church 69
Troubling Verses for the Church 70
- The Mystery of God 70
- The Covenant: Daniel 9:27 73
- The Covenant: Psalm 83:3-8 74
- No Man Knows: Matthew 24:36 75
- The Raptured Church: Revelation 7:9-17 75

The Great Falling Away 76
- The Declaration: 2 Thessalonians 2:3 76
- The Third Trumpet: Revelation 8:10-11 77
- Message to the Church at Thyatira: Revelation 2:18-29 77

Two Doctrines 80
- The Imminent Return of Christ: A False Church Doctrine 80
- Resurrections 83
- About This Time Line 88

The Calculations 94

CHAPTER 5
NOTES ON DANIEL 11 95
Preface to Daniel 11 95
The Text of Daniel 11 97

Table of Contents

The Rise of the False Prophet 104
The Rise of the Antichrist 107
Judgment on the Antichrist 111
The Abomination That Maketh Desolate 112
The People Who Know Their God: The Two
Witnesses 114
The King 114
AUTHOR'S TESTIMONY 127

Foreword

Jesus Is Coming—A Different Perspective is the product of more than thirty years of study. In my younger years, I was content to accept the words of my elders without researching the scriptures for myself. One day, Leonard Cleaver, a mature Christian friend, challenged me to prove what I had spiritually learned in my walk. I searched, studied and became very frustrated! Leonard's every challenge caused me to grow in the increased knowledge of God's Word. I discovered that some widely accepted positions regarding end-time theology did not have the solid bases and were not as correct as I had previously thought.

Many notes and smaller essays written over the years have gone into this book to create its finished product. I have attempted to cohesively represent a document of intense study and clarity on the subject of the end times. It is my hope that you will grow in greater knowledge and understanding of the role you will play in the end-time Church.

Ervin L. Steele

CHAPTER 1

TWO PREMISES REGARDING THE LORD'S IMMINENT RETURN

Jesus Is Coming: A Different Perspective (the Premise Stated)

Where the Church is Today

For more than 50 years, there has been ridicule in the Church for those who attempt to give a specific day for our Lord's appearance. Some say, *Shame on those individuals who are presumptuous enough to state a date.* Others quote our Lord's words, *No man knows the day or the hour.* When our Lord said these words, He was always careful to encourage watchfulness and awareness (Mark 13:37). I believe the Lord knew that only the end-of-the-age Christians could and would know that date before it happened and that He wanted all in the Church for the past two thousand years to have the blessed hope of His coming for them in their hearts. This hope, gained through the study of His Word and a result of the heart's desire to be taken out of tribulation and trials, was the reason many early Christians were martyred. Actively searching the scriptures, understanding the timing of His return, and maintaining the blessed hope given in Titus 2:11-13 would have a permanent effect on all those who did so. The Apostle John made it very clear in 1 John 3:3, *And every man that hath this hope in him purifieth himself even as He is pure.* This blessed hope will continue until the end of the age. The Lord said, *Go ye therefore, and teach all nations...teaching them to observe all things whatsoever I have commanded you: and lo, I am with you always, even unto the end of the age* (Matthew 28:19-20). Though there seems to be a contradiction between our Lord's declaration, *No man knows,"* and Paul's declaration in 1 Thessalonians 5:4-9, *But ye, brethren, are not in darkness, that that day should overtake you as a thief,* the scriptures convinced me that the Church can and will know this day before it is fulfilled.

There are, however, several false doctrines taught to the Church that prevent the Church from having a clear understanding of the Lord's return. One such doctrine is that all scriptures have been fulfilled concerning the Church, so our exit is imminent. This is not true. The Church is also taught that they will not go through the Great Tribulation. This is only partially true. My studies have taught me that the Great Tribulation is a period of time which begins 30 days before the middle of the 70th week with the

Chapter 1

setting up of an idol in a holy place, and it will end 75 days after the resurrection on the 1335th day of the 70th week. There are other false doctrines that I will not dwell on here but will cover in the following chapters. They will become obvious after one understands what I am attempting to teach.

There are doctrines that should but are not being taught concerning what the difference between the Armageddon battle and the Gog-Magog battle is. Our Lord clearly taught in Luke 17:29-30 that the Resurrection Day is also the Day of Wrath. The Church is not being taught the true severity of the Day of Wrath nor that the Resurrection-Wrath Day is an appointed day. Scripture teaches that there will be 144,000 Jews sealed. Contrary to what is being taught, they are sealed so they will survive the Day of Wrath, not to preach for 3-1/2 or seven years.

That is enough of this brief description of where the Church is today. In the following chapters, I will attempt, with God's help, to give you concrete events to look for and also the exact day (not dates) the scriptures teach for the return of the Lord.

The Seven Feasts of the Lord

The seven feasts of the Lord, outlined in Leviticus 23, are a blueprint for God's dealing with mankind. The seven feasts are divided into two groups. In the first group of feasts, three occur in the month of Nissan, and the fourth occurs 50 days after the third feast. This first group of feasts represents the finished work of Christ, demonstrating His birth, burial, and resurrection; and its application to us in our redemption and communion with Him. There is then a long period between the first group of feasts and the second group of feasts. This period is the Church Age, and we are in its closing days. The second group consists of three feasts that will bring mankind to the consummation of God's plan—a new heaven and a new earth.

The feasts of our Lord were and are appointed days. It all started in Genesis 15:13-16, *And he said unto Abram, "Know of a surety that thy seed shall be a stranger in a land that is not theirs, and shall serve them...and also that nation, whom they shall serve, will I judge: and afterward shall they come out with great substance. And thou shalt go to thy fathers in peace; thou shalt be buried in a good old age. But in the fourth generation they shall come hither again; for the iniquity of the Amorites is not yet full."*

This declaration from God began the process that would lead to the commandments of the feasts recorded in Leviticus. Each feast would be celebrated on an exact day in the fullness of God's timing. Thus, Passover was to be celebrated on the 14th day of Nissan, forever. On the 15th day of Nissan, the unleavened bread feast was to be celebrated, forever. The next feast becomes more exacting.

When they come into the land which I give unto you and shall reap the harvest thereof, then ye shall bring a sheaf of the first fruits of your harvest unto the priest, and he shall wave the sheaf before the Lord, to be

Chapter 1

accepted for you: on the next day after the Sabbath the priest shall wave it.

Leviticus 23:10-11

Let us stop here and get some perspective of what is being presented. This feast, observed in the same week as the feast of unleavened bread, was held on the 16th day of the first month, Nissan. It would coincide with the beginning of the barley harvest. It becomes very obvious to us Christians that this feast speaks of resurrection and of Christ as the first fruit. Paul wrote in 1 Corinthians 15:20, *But now is Christ risen from the dead and become the first fruits of them that slept.* Thus, Christ was the fulfillment of the wave-sheaf offering and feast.

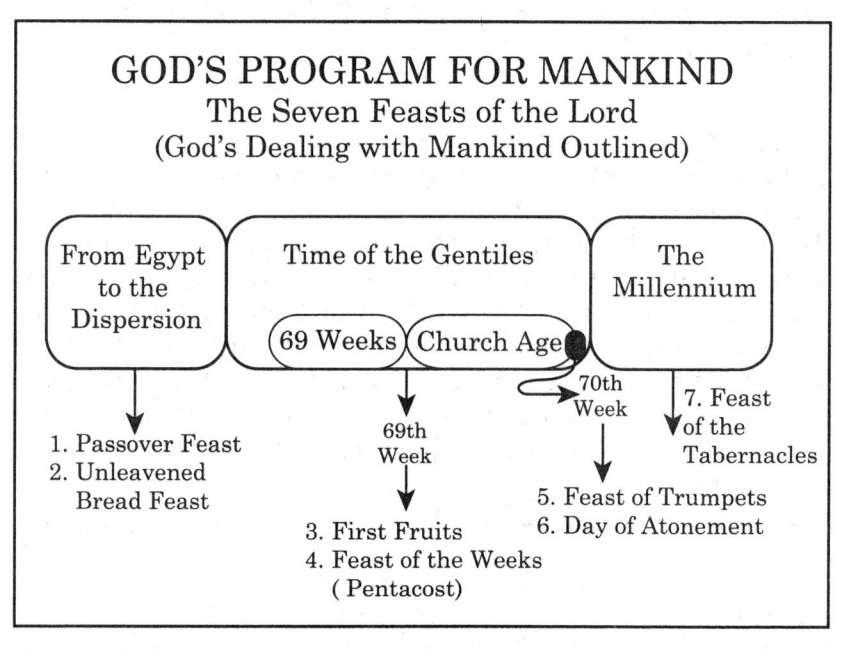

GOD'S PROGRAM FOR MANKIND
The Seven Feasts of the Lord
(God's Dealing with Mankind Outlined)

```
From Egypt          Time of the Gentiles              The
to the                                             Millennium
Dispersion        ( 69 Weeks )( Church Age )
                                          ↘ 70th
        ↓              ↓                    Week      ↓ 7. Feast
  1. Passover Feast  69th                              of the
  2. Unleavened      Week                    ↓         Tabernacles
     Bread Feast      ↓              5. Feast of Trumpets
                  3. First Fruits    6. Day of Atonement
                  4. Feast of the Weeks
                     (Pentacost)
```

The above seven feasts are divided into two groups. In the first group of feasts, three occur in the month of Nissan, and the fourth, fifty days after the third feast. This first group of feasts represents the finished works of Christ. There is then a long period between the first group of feasts and the second group of feasts. This period is the Church Age, in which we find ourselves in its closing days. The second group consists of three feasts that will bring mankind to the Consummation (a new heaven and a new earth). In the above diagram, these feasts have been placed in time as their actual fulfillment.

Chapter 1

Pentecost and Wave-Loaves Offering

And ye shall count unto you from the morrow after the sabbath, from the day that ye brought the sheaf of the wave offering; seven sabbaths shall be complete: Even unto the morrow after the seventh sabbath shall ye number fifty days; and ye shall offer a new meal offering unto the Lord. Ye shall bring out of your habitations two wave loaves of two tenth parts; they shall be of fine flour; they shall be baken with leaven; they are the firstfruits unto the Lord.

Leviticus 23:15

Following the instructions in this verse, I counted, in the years from 1995 to 2000, seven Sabbaths to Pentecost. After the year 2000, one cannot count seven Sabbaths to Pentecost. It always takes eight weeks to get to the 50 days. Why? I don't know! Pentecost, of course, brought the birth of the Church. From that very precise day, the Wave-Loaves offering began.

For two thousand years from Pentecost to the Resurrection-Wrath Day, all deceased believers rise to heavenly mansions where they await the resurrection. Why are there two loaves in this offering? My impulse leads me to believe that they represent the two remaining resurrections. There are three resurrections: (1) the Lord's resurrection, (2) the resurrection of those who are His at His coming, and (3) the final resurrection which occurs a thousand years later. The last resurrection will see multitudes entering the Kingdom of God.

Jesus Is Coming—A Different Perspective

At this same time, the damned appear before the Great White Throne of Judgment. They will kneel before the Savior and proclaim Him Lord of all. Please stop now and read John 5:25-29. I believe these verses portray the order of the resurrection given in 1 Corinthians 15. I also believe that these two loaves represent only the second resurrection. The third resurrection will occur at the consummation of the new heaven and the new earth and will end the last feast, the Feast of Tabernacles. Again the question, why two loaves representing this resurrection? When the second resurrection occurs, the Lord will go forth from the third heaven and gather the ascending Church from the second heaven.

As He continues to descend, the saints from the second heaven and the Lord meet the ascending Church (those who are still alive on the earth) in the air. Thus, the Lord will come with all His saints. Since the raptured Church is described in Revelation 7:13-17, it is clear that they have been taken out of the Great Tribulation. Please reread my explanation of the Great Tribulation on page one. I must hasten to say the Bible does not teach a 3-1/2 or seven-year Great Tribulation period.

To answer why two loaves, I must go back to the words *"those who are His at His coming."* It could well be that the Old Testament believers would be included in one of the loaves. I am sure that Elijah and Moses would be counted as His. They certainly were with Him at the transfiguration. Then there is John the Baptist, the friend of the Bridegroom. It certainly would not violate scripture if these Old Testament

Chapter 1

saints are included in *"those who are His at His coming."* Please stop and read Revelation 11:18. It should be made clear the wave-loaves offering begins with Pentecost. It will end when the seventh trumpet begins to sound. The last trumpet will fall on the first day of Tishri, fulfilling the Feast of Trumpets ceremony. Proof that this is the Resurrection-Wrath Day is given in Daniel 12. The 70th week will come to an end 1260 days later, on the 14th day of Nissan, the Passover Feast. On this day the temple will be made holy by God's anointing.

A few years ago, I heard a theologian declare that at the rapture there would be as many believers alive on Earth as all those who preceded them. I do not know who this man was, but I recently heard this statement again on Billy Graham's "Day of Decision" program.

The Feast of Trumpets

And the Lord spake unto Moses, saying, speak unto the children of Israel, saying In the seventh month, in the first day of the month, shall ye have a sabbath, a memorial of blowing of trumpets, an holy convocation. Ye shall do no servile work therein: but ye shall offer an offering made by fire unto the Lord.
Leviticus 23:23-25

This scripture gives the date of the Feast of Trumpets as the first day of the seventh month. This feast, as the prior ones, will soon have its fulfillment on the day assigned with the sound of the last trumpet. This day will be the Resurrection-Wrath Day! In the year 2000, this day fell on September 30th. In 2001, it fell on September 18th. The question I ask myself is, "Will the first six trumpets occur before the 18th day of September this year? Two of the trumpets, the second and fourth, should be quite apparent to Christians all over the earth. The second trumpet will cause a great explosion in the sea, destroying a third of the ships on the sea and a third of life in the sea, and a third part of the sea will turn red. We Christians will experience this. At the fourth trumpet, the whole earth will be darkened for eight hours. An event, which will occur 3-1/2 days before the Resurrection-Wrath Day, will be the two witnesses (Christians and Jews) lying dead in the streets of Jerusalem. Another event that will occur before the Feast of Trumpets day is the setting up of the idol in the holy place. All of these events should keep the Church from being surprised at our Lord's coming. There should be no Christian caught unawares or as a thief in the night. Please study the sample time line in Chapter 4 of this book for further clarification.

The seventh trumpet will bring an end to *"the mystery of God"*, detailed in Ephesians 3:1-12, and the end of the age (Revelation 10:7). At this time, definite changes occur in God's programs. The day of grace will end with our rapture and thrones of judgment will be set up (Daniel 7 and Revelation 11:18). So far, I have dwelt on the positive side of this appointed day. Now we will begin with the appointed day in Daniel that leads to the wrath of God. Three quotations in Daniel refer to the appointed day: (1) In Daniel 8:19, the angel said, *Behold, I will make thee know what shall be in the last end of the indignation: for at the time appointed the end shall be.* (2) Daniel 11:27 states, *And*

Chapter 1

both these kings' hearts shall be to do mischief, and they shall speak lies at one table; but it shall not prosper: for yet the end shall be at the time appointed. (3) Daniel 11:35 states, *And some of them of understanding shall fall, to try them, and to purge, and to make them white, even to the time of the end: because it is yet for a time appointed.* Remember Matthew 28:20 (NKJV), which we looked at earlier: *Lo, I am with you always even unto the end of the age.* The "end" these verses refer to will occur after the Church goes through the tribulation of the first six trumpets. After the fourth trumpet, the idol is set up, and the Church will go through 30 days of great tribulation. We are taken out of the Great Tribulation when the seventh trumpet begins to sound. It is then that God's wrath will be dispensed. Those who survive this Day of Wrath and are able to sustain life and reach the 1335th day of the 70th week will go into the new millennium. The horrible events that occur on this appointed day are recorded in the sixth seal and the seventh trumpet. Contrary to popular opinion, all these bowls of wrath will occur in one day, not in 3-1/2 years.

Many Christians do not realize the severity of God's wrath. Armageddon occurs with missiles flying all over the earth, destroying many major population centers. After this action, God intervenes. He will shake the heavens and the earth, which will result in huge hailstones and great tidal waves. Today we have six billion people on earth. Within an hour or so, after the earth is moved out of its place, I doubt that one billion will be left. The population that is in the interior of the large continents will be those who will remain. Many of this remainder will make up the Gog-

Magog army that is recorded in Ezekiel. They will be destroyed in the mountains of Judah. This battle will occur on the 2300th day of the 70th week, ending the "time of the Gentiles." Actually, I believe that the time of the Gentiles ends with the end of the age, but God will demonstrate its end decisively approximately three years later with this battle.

Before moving onto another topic, it is important for the reader to understand the connection I see between the Feast of Trumpets and Rosh Hashanah, the Jewish New Year's Day, both of which occur on the first day of the seventh month. The connection I see is that the Feast of Trumpets ends a period of time; Rosh Hashanah represents the beginning of the new civil year, a new period of time.

The Day of Atonement

And the Lord spoke unto Moses, saying, also on the tenth day of this seventh month there shall be a day of atonement: it shall be an holy convocation unto you; and ye shall afflict your souls, and offer an offering made by fire unto the Lord.

Leviticus 23:26-27

It will be at least three years after the literal fulfillment of the Feast of Trumpets that the Day of Atonement will be fulfilled. Its appointed day, the tenth day of the seventh month, will be after the 2300th day, in whatever year it is to be accomplished. This Day of Atonement, I believe, will be marked by the realization that they have been delivered. Very

Chapter 1

few, if any, will have perished through the process of the trumpets and the Gog-Magog battle. The gathering-together process and the building of the temple will bring about a national unity. They will see God's hands working on their behalf. True repentance will occur, and they will call upon Jesus. They will be able to see the literal fulfillment of Revelation 12:13-17.

How the 70th Week Ends

When the 2300th day occurs, there will be 220 days to the end of the 70th week. It is important to understand the scriptures and events that bring a conclusion to the 70th week. The events that will occur up to Passover are quite revealing. The cleansing of the land, temple, and people must be accomplished, with the cleansing of the temple occurring first. The building of the temple will start soon after the Resurrection-Wrath Day. The temple must be built, cleansed, and anointed before the 70th week ends on the Passover Feast. To understand this, we must go back to Daniel 9:24, which states, *Seventy weeks are determined upon thy people and upon thy holy city, to finish the transgression, and to make an end of sins, and to make reconciliation for iniquity, and to bring in everlasting righteousness, and to seal up the vision and prophecy; and to anoint the most Holy.* The last thing on this list of things that must be done is the anointing of the most Holy. Many would say this occurred when John the Baptist baptized the Lord, and the Holy Spirit anointed Him. I, of course, believe that literally happened, but I do not believe that this verse is referring to the anointing of Jesus. I believe that the temple is being referred to here. Before the 70th week ends, the temple will be cleansed and then anointed. It will be visually apparent that the glory of God is present there, with a cloud over the temple by day and a pillar of fire at night. Ezekiel 43:1-5 describes the anointing. The glory fills not only the most Holy, but every room in the house. This is what I think the Lord was referring to when He said in Ezekiel 39:12-13, *And seven months shall the house of Israel be burying them, that they may cleanse the land. Yea, all the people of the land shall bury them; and it shall be to them a renown the day that I shall be glorified, saith the Lord God.* The cleansing of the land will be completed at least three days after the temple. All the people of the land are commissioned to cleanse the land, and thus they are all defiled and must be cleansed. (For more information on this, read all of Numbers 19.) During the 220 days from the 2300th day to the Feast of Passover, God will finish all visions and prophecies that must be "sealed up" (Daniel 9:24) before the 70th week can be ended. Among the events that are to be completed: (1) Satan will be cast into the bottomless pit, (2) the Day of Atonement will occur, (3) Daniel 12:11 will be fulfilled, (4) the temple will be cleansed, as seen in Ezekiel 45:18, (5) the most Holy will be anointed, and (6) the people will be cleansed, and they will experience a true Passover, both spiritually and physically, as they call upon the Lord.

The Feast of Tabernacles

And the Lord spake unto Moses saying, "Speak unto the children of Israel, saying, the fifteenth day of this

Chapter 1

seventh month shall be the feast of tabernacles for seven days unto the Lord. On the first day shall be an holy convocation: ye shall do no servile work therein. Seven days ye shall offer an offering made by fire unto the Lord: on the eighth day shall be a holy convocation unto you; and ye shall offer an offering made by fire unto the Lord: it is a solemn assembly; and ye shall do no servile work therein."

Leviticus 23:33-36

Just as all the above feasts of the Lord had their literal fulfillment on the appointed day, thus shall it be with the Feast of Tabernacles. This feast will begin on the 15th day of Tishri following the completion of the 70th week, and it will be celebrated for a thousand years. Multitudes from all the nations will go up to Jerusalem to seek out the Lord their God. This feast will culminate with the third resurrection and the consummation.

In the Fullness of Time
(the Premise Restated)

The Servant

Behold my servant, whom I uphold; mine elect, in whom my soul delighteth; I have put my spirit upon him: he shall bring forth judgment to the Gentiles. He shall not cry, nor lift up, nor cause his voice to be heard in the street. A bruised reed shall he not break, and the smoking flax shall he not quench: he shall bring forth

judgment unto truth. He shall not fail nor be discouraged, till he have set judgment in the earth: and the isles shall wait for his law. Thus saith God the Lord, he that created the heavens, and stretched them out; he who spread forth the earth, and that which cometh out of it; he that giveth breath unto the people upon it, and spirit to them that walk therein: I the Lord have called thee in righteousness, and will hold thine hand, and will keep thee, and give thee for a covenant of the people, for a light of the Gentiles.
Isaiah 42:1-6

But when the fullness of the time was come, God sent forth his Son, made of a woman, made under the law, to redeem them that were under the law, that we might receive the adoption of sons.
Galatians 4:4-5

Let this mind be in you, which was also in Jesus Christ: who, being in the form of God, thought it not robbery to be equal with God: But made himself of no reputation, and took upon him the form of a servant, and was made in the likeness of men: And being found in fashion as a man, he humbled himself, and became obedient unto death, even the death of the cross.
Philippians 2:5-8

In the approximately two thousand years since the birth of our Savior, the above scriptures have been accomplished. Our Lord's intercessory prayer, given the day before He went to the cross and recorded in John 17:4, begins with the Lord stating to the Father, *I have finished the work that you gavest me to do.* For 33 years, He functioned in His human capacity, fulfilling the law and becoming the Lamb of God that

Chapter 1

taketh away the sins of the world. In the last 3-1/2 years of His life, He began His ministry of preaching the Kingdom of God and establishing the foundation of the Church through the apostles.

In Daniel 9:26, it was declared that in the fullness of time the Messiah would be cut off, ending the 69th week of the seventy weeks given to the Hebrews to fulfill. The fulfillment of the 69th week occurred when the Lord was crucified on the 14th day of Nissan in the year that He died. On this particular Passover, God also established a new covenant for all people (Isaiah 42:6). Paul declares in 1 Corinthians 5:7-8, *Purge out therefore the old leaven, that ye may be a new lump, as ye are unleavened. For even Christ our Passover is sacrificed for us: Therefore let us keep the feast, not with old leaven, neither with the leaven of malice and wickedness; but with the unleavened bread of sincerity and truth.* Thus, with the fullness of time three days later, the First Fruits Feast was transformed into the first resurrection. Paul declared in 1 Corinthians 15:20, *But now is Christ risen from the dead, and become the firstfruits of them that slept.* With this resurrection, the feasts of the Lord as recorded in Leviticus 23 began a process in which two more resurrections are to be fulfilled in the fullness of time. It was through these Jewish feasts that God was revealing how He would accomplish the two remaining resurrections. God, through the Jews, would graft into these Jewish feasts the process wherein multitudes throughout the world would participate in the second resurrection (the first being the Lord's). This process, later to be called the dispensation of grace, was given a definite path of development beginning with the feast of Pentecost.

Fifty days after the first resurrection, the Church would come into being. The development of the Church was given a definite outline for the various stages to be accomplished. Ten days before Pentecost, at our Lord's ascension, He announced to the believers who assembled to witness His departure, *But ye shall receive power, after that the Holy Ghost is come upon you: and ye shall be witnesses unto me both in Jerusalem, and in all Judaea, and in Samaria, and unto the uttermost part of the earth* (Acts 1:8). Pentecost would have its completion with the second resurrection, which would include two definite groups of people. In 1 Corinthians 15, they are called those who are Christ's at His coming. They are represented in the feast of Pentecost as two leavened loaves of bread presented to God the Father. These two loaves are the Church and the Old Testament Jews who put their faith in the blood of the Lamb and believed God's Word. Blessed are they who participate in this first resurrection, because the second death has no power over them.

Those who will participate in the second resurrection but who are not part of the Church were represented as a group at the transfiguration by Moses and Elias (Matthew 17:2 and Mark 9:2). In the fullness of time, God has already established this loaf (people). The Lord's resurrection was the first resurrection of those who are already dead who are His. The second loaf that will be presented to the Father is still in the process of development. This loaf includes both Jews and Gentiles (the Church), and after two thousand years of development, it will have its completion when the Feasts of Trumpets is completed. This will occur on the first day of the seventh month on the Jewish calendar in

Chapter 1

the near future. (For a brief description of these two loaves, read Galatians, Chapter three.)

Paul declares in 1 Corinthians 15:51-52 and in 1 Thessalonians 4:16 that we are resurrected at the last trumpet. Three and one half years before the trumpet occurs, God grafts the nation of Israel back into the feasts of the Lord. After the last trumpet is completed, it will, once again, become God's main focus. The 69th week of the 70 weeks ended at the crucifixion. The 70th week begins 3-1/2 years before our resurrection, and it will end on the Feast of Passover, 1260 days after the Feast of Trumpets or the Resurrection-Wrath Day. God will not initiate a new covenant with the nation of Israel until the completion of the 70th week. One of the conditions for the ending of the 70th week is that all unfulfilled scripture and prophecies about Israel must be fulfilled (Daniel 9:24). God declares in Jeremiah 31:31, Ezekiel 24:25, and Ezekiel 37:26-28 that a new covenant of peace will be given to the Israelites. The end of the 70th week will bring the beginning of the Feast of Tabernacles; this feast will have its beginnings on the 15th day of the seventh month in a year soon after the end of the 70th week.

With the fullness of time approximately one thousand years later, the third resurrection will also bring about the final death. This death involves the separation of the spirit from the soul. Those who are damned will go into the lake of fire. Those who are resurrected into life will inherit a new earth. Thus, with the completion of all these things in the fullness of time, time shall be no more.

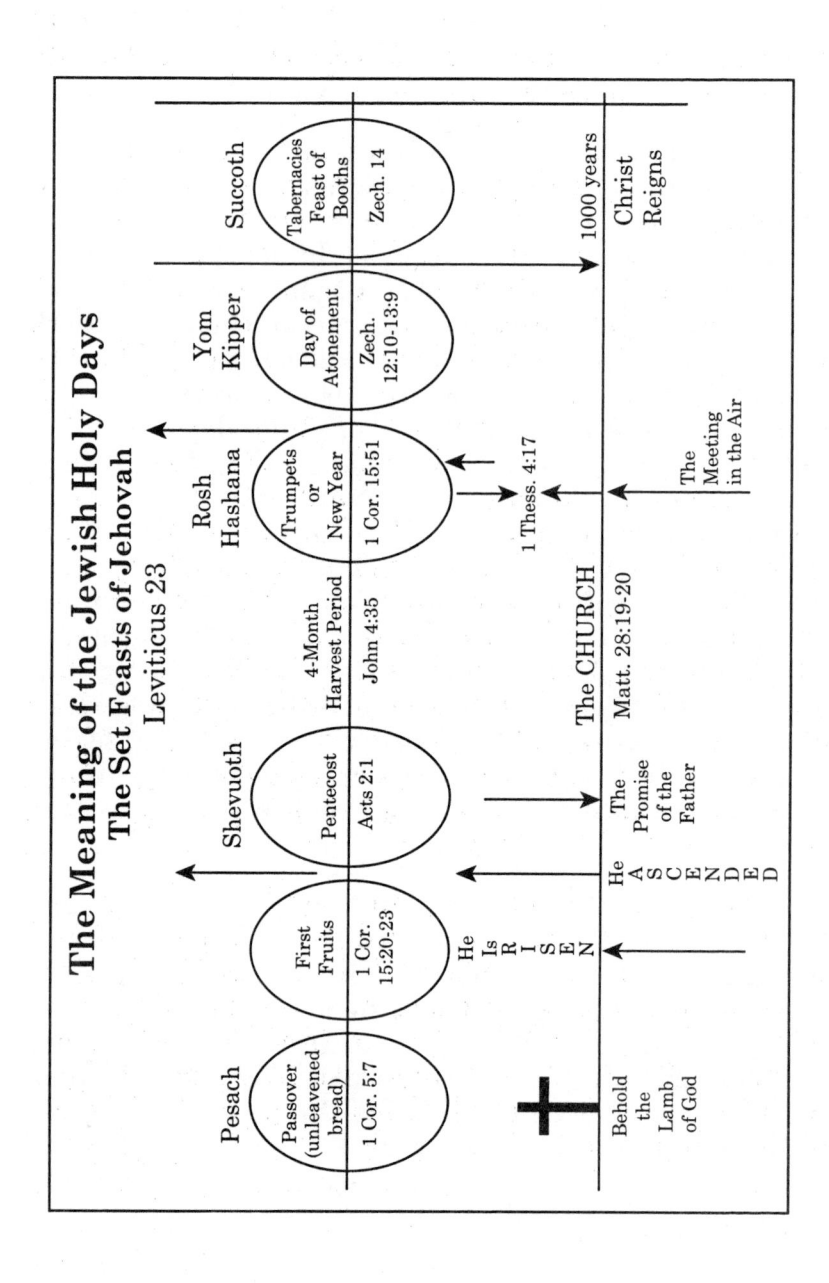

The Meaning of the Jewish Holy Days
The Set Feasts of Jehovah
Leviticus 23

Pesach	First Fruits	Shevuoth	4-Month Harvest Period	Rosh Hashana	Yom Kippur	Succoth
Passover (unleavened bread)	1 Cor. 15:20-23	Pentecost	John 4:35	Trumpets or New Year	Day of Atonement	Tabernacles Feast of Booths
1 Cor. 5:7		Acts 2:1		1 Cor. 15:51	Zech. 12:10-13:9	Zech. 14

He Is RISEN

He ASCENDED

The Promise of the Father

1 Thess. 4:17

The CHURCH — Matt. 28:19-20

Behold the Lamb of God

✝

The Meeting in the Air

1000 years — Christ Reigns

CHAPTER 2

WATCHFULNESS IN VIEW OF THE RETURN OF OUR LORD

For the Son of man is as a man taking a far journey, who left his house, and gave authority to his servants, and to every man his work, and commanded the porter to watch. Watch ye therefore: for ye know not when the master of the house cometh, at even, or at midnight, or at the cockcrowing, or in the morning. Lest coming suddenly he find you sleeping. And what I say unto you say unto all, watch.

Mark 13:34-37

The first chapter revealed the outline that God is using to deal with mankind. This outline runs from the birth of the Church to the consummation (creation of a new heaven and a new earth). Our participation in this outline is included from Pentecost to the Feast of Trumpets. The Church can look back at two thousand years of history. It is now that time in which our Lord's return will soon occur. As such, our Lord's command to watch is of paramount importance. The text of this chapter deals with the "end-time" Church and the events to watch for before it is resurrected.

Events That Must Occur Before the Resurrection

In Revelation 3:14-19, our Lord addressed the apostate church. When He returns for His Church, He will find a multitude of professing Christians. These He has divided into the true church and the apostate church. The apostate church has not received our Lord with repentance and saving knowledge. They have not been "born again."

Our salvation is through faith. The scriptures declare that this faith is a gift from God (Ephesians 2:8). Though He has been absent from this earthly scene for nearly two thousand years, our Savior currently sits at the right hand of God. When one hears the Gospel and believes, he is given faith. What one does with this faith is crucial. At some point while using this faith, power enters the individual via the Holy Spirit, and he becomes "born again". John 1:12 declares, *But as many as received him, to them gave he power to become the sons of God, even to them that believe on his name.* While exercising this power upon the faith received, an individual becomes known by Jesus. Jesus declared to those who would do this that they, as individuals, could do nothing without Him, thus ensuring a relationship with Him. There are

Chapter 2

those who hear the Gospel and receive faith, but deception takes over them, and their works do not glorify the Savior. Their works lift them up to their own glory. They do not receive the Holy Spirit and become children of God. They do not repent of their sins. They do not come to know their Savior in a personal way. These our Lord addresses at the end of the age, *I never knew you: depart from me, ye that work iniquity* (Matthew 7:23 and Luke 13:27). The parable of the talents in Matthew 25 illustrates what has been just declared to you. Here, the master goes to a far country. He gives talents (faith through the written word) for his servants to use while he is gone. The servants glorified their master during his absence by using the talents that were given. With this process, a relationship develops between the servant and the master. Our Lord explains how He will deal with both of these groups of professing Christians in Matthew 13:37-43. John also describes this very thing in Revelation 14:14-20.

The book of Revelation adds to this understanding. To bring the Church to the end of this age, God has given us seals and trumpets. The seals are a broad view of the development of end-time conditions on earth before our Lord appears at the sixth seal. The sixth seal includes six trumpets that must be accomplished before our Lord's appearance at the seventh trumpet. Details of the trumpets are given in Chapter 3 of this book. Here, a description of the seals would be helpful:

- **The first seal** describes the Church going triumphantly to the end of the age.

- **The second seal** describes communism going forth, taking peace from the earth. This movement will continue, mainly through Russia and China, to the end of the age.

- **The third seal** describes world famine brought about by economic conditions. These economic controls established during the second seal period, will directly or indirectly contributed to wars and civil wars. These wars, coupled with natural disasters like drought, earthquakes, and hurricanes, will have a profound effect on world economics.

- **The fourth seal** describes death. World conditions, both political and physical, will bring on a continual display of human suffering, culminating with death and destruction of those who reject the first seal.

- **The fifth seal** departs from this earthly scene. It depicts the martyred under the altar in heaven crying for justice to God the Father.

- **The sixth seal** describes the process of God's justice (judgment) in seven trumpets.

The first seal and the first trumpet are dealing with Church development to the end of the age. We must be here until the end of the age (Matthew 28:20). We must be here when the idol is set up in the holy place 1230 days into the 70th week. We must be here when the last trumpet begins to sound (Revelation 11:15 and 1 Corinthians 15). During the second and third trumpets, there is war going on in the second heaven.

Chapter 2

At this time, the false professing Christians in heaven are separated and bundled to be burned in the lake of fire. When the fourth trumpet sounds, Satan and his angels are cast from heaven to the earth, but the bundled "tares" (the false professing Christians) will not be cast to the earth until the seventh trumpet sounds. It is then that God will shake the heavens and the earth (Revelation 6:13, Revelation 16:17-21, and Isaiah 13:13). From the third to the seventh trumpet, God is separating, on earth, the remaining true and false believers. This will result in a great falling away from the true Church (2 Thessalonians 2:3). The true Church will overcome Satan and his followers by the word of their testimony and the blood of the Lamb (Revelation 12:11). At the seventh trumpet, the true Church is taken out, leaving the false professing Church, the Laodicean Church, to go through God's wrath and be cast into the lake of fire. People continually ask, "How long will this period of the trumpets be?" The answer, based on Daniel 12 and Revelation 11:3, is 3-1/2 years, when God once again starts dealing with Israel and the 70th week begins. Daniel 12:6 states, *And one said to the man clothed in linen, which was upon the waters of the river, How long shall it be to the end of these wonders?* The wonders referred to here are those things that are mentioned in Daniel 11 and 12. In Daniel 12:7 the man upon the waters declares, *...it shall be for a time, times, and an half; and when he shall have accomplished to scatter the power of the holy people, all these things shall be finished.* Connecting these things with the New Testament and the trumpets of Revelation is quite revealing.

Probable Events That Will Occur Before the Resurrection

The second trumpet could be a nuclear device in the sea. This will result in the destruction of a third of the United States' naval carrier fleet (probably in the Persian Gulf). The immediate reaction to this will be the fulfillment of Daniel 11:5-9. The king of the south in these verses is that person who heads the United Nations. The prince that is stronger is the United States. The fortress of the king of the north is Iran.

After or during the completion of the activities described in these verses, I believe the third trumpet "Wormwood" will occur. Part of this trumpet will be accomplished when the king of the south's daughter (the world's economic system), currently centered in the United States, crumbles. The process of the control of the world economics will start moving to the land of Shinar mentioned in Zechariah 5:5-11. The United States will withdraw from the Middle East and put its influence behind the United Nations—the king of the south.

Russia, having lost Iran's influence in the Middle East will engage in a blitz operation in the Middle East, even advancing toward Egypt. The Russian objective will be to release Iran's leaders, gods, and treasures (Daniel 11:40-43). Before the Russian blitz reaches Egypt, a ten-nation confederation of Arabs will react in the Middle East to eliminate the Russian influence over them. The False Prophet and/or the Antichrist will successfully keep the Russians from returning through the Middle East and subjugating

Chapter 2

them like they did parts of Europe 50 years earlier. The United Nations will probably join the confederation to stop the Russians. During this period, the False Prophet will fall and not be found. The Antichrist will take over the confederation, and this power will make Israel subservient to him. He will have the backing of the European Union and the United Nations, to a degree.

Meanwhile, unbeknownst to the world, the war in heaven will be culminated and the fourth and fifth trumpets will occur. The eight hours of darkness that is a result of the fourth trumpet will cover the Earth and leave many wondering. Because of the sudden influx of power from the confederation, the Antichrist will become more militant and anti-God. When the ships of Cyprus, where the Russians have a huge naval base, come against him, he will be saddened and will return to his headquarters in Hebron. There he will confer with the leadership of Arabs and apostate Jews. I speculate it will be at this time that an assassination attempt will be made on his life. He will be close to death. Suddenly, the False Prophet, who had fallen and could not be found, will step forward and heal the Antichrist. This healing will not be complete, and he will remain blind in his right eye and paralyzed in one of his arms. Perhaps it is during this assassination attempt that the fourth trumpet occurs, thus intensifying the drama of the hour. When the False Prophet appears, he will be in-dwelt by Satan, who has been cast down.

From the second trumpet up to this time, the world's economic condition will be in shambles. The powers that exist will be unstable, and great fear will cover the earth. The United States' leadership will be completely committed to the establishment of a one-world government through the United Nations. A worldwide depression will exist, and people will be looking for leadership that does not appear to be forthcoming.

I believe that from the fourth trumpet (darkness) to the Day of Judgment (Armageddon), there will be much tribulation, the primary cause of which will be Satan's direct hand in world events. He will perform various miracles. He will plot to maintain control of the Middle East through the Antichrist and will plot to eliminate world powers desiring this control. He will plot to establish a new world religion by combining the three major world religions. In doing this, he will try to control the world economic system (Babylon) by requiring everyone to take his mark and to worship the image that will be set up in the synagogue in Hebron (the holy place). From the placement of this idol to the Resurrection-Wrath Day will be 30 days of Great Tribulation. For some details of Satan's plotting, read Isaiah 28:14-22, noting especially verses 15, 18, and 22. The overflowing scourge mentioned in verses 15 and 18 will be the kings of the east.

Chapter 2

An Event That Will Occur Before the Resurrection

The Commission

In the near future, an open door will be given to part of the end-time Church. They will have the honor to act in the place of our Lord. As the body of Christ, they will fulfill our Lord's commission to declare the "day of vengeance" given in Isaiah 61:2. They will do this because they are witnesses for our Lord. To be a witness is the destiny of all those who have been "born again." Our Lord passed this privilege onto the Church when He commissioned the apostle John to do so in Revelation 10:8-11. The spirit of love that was so pervasive in John will take hold of the Philadelphian Church and thus fulfill our Lord's words to Peter in John 21:18-23. This privilege will be in effect during the last persecution period of the Church, which will strengthen its witness. Daniel 12:7 states that the power of the holy people is scattered.

I believe that the third trumpet of Revelation 8:10-11 is directly related to this scattering of the power of the holy people. At this time, the Antichrist will be given power to make war with the saints and to overcome them (Revelation 14:7). As this process is taking place, the Philadelphian Church will be overcoming Satan spiritually as Revelation 12:11 states, *by the blood of the Lamb and by the word of their testimony; and they loved not their lives unto the death.* All of this will have its culmination when the two witnesses lie dead in the streets of Jerusalem.

Wormwood, the third trumpet, will separate false believers from true believers. In this process, the Laodicean Church will be spewed out by our Lord. During this period, Daniel 11:32-35 will also be fulfilled.

The Commission Given: Revelation 10

My brief interpretation of this chapter in Revelation is the following: John sees the glorified Christ as an angel with His right foot upon the sea and His left foot on the earth. In His hand He holds a little book. When He speaks, seven thunders say things that are not to be known, and a voice from heaven (the Father) commands that these thunders be sealed. Jesus then makes a declaration, *But in the days of the voice of the seventh angel; when he shall begin to sound, the mystery of God should be finished, as he hath declared to his servants the prophets* (Revelation 10:7). God the Father then instructs John to take the little book out of the angel's hand, and eat it up, and it was in his mouth sweet as honey; and as soon as he had eaten it, his belly was bitter. And He (Jesus) said unto me, *Thou must prophesy again before many peoples, and nations, and tongues, and kings* (Revelation 10:11).

That this, indeed, is a commission given to John can be substantiated by comparing scripture with scripture. In the book of Ezekiel, Ezekiel is also given a commission. He was given a roll to eat. It, too, was sweet in his mouth and bitter in his belly. The message

Chapter 2

John is to give is to be given before the day of vengeance, before the seventh angel is to sound (Revelation 10:7). When John was given this commission, he was quite advanced in age and exiled on the isle of Patmos. He was definitely to be a witness before many peoples, nations, tongues, and kings. John went home to heaven soon after receiving this commission. The mystery of God is finished when the seventh angel begins to sound. This mystery is the process of the continuous building of the Church. It begins with the Gospel, the person of Jesus and His ministry. When one receives Jesus and His Gospel, he receives the power of the Holy Spirit that Jesus gives to those who believe in Him. The people who believe on Him then use that power to reach others. For two thousand years, this process has been going on. This process is the mystery hidden in God, and it has brought multitudes into the kingdom of God through the grace given to the Church.

During our Lord's earthly ministry, He read in the synagogue of Nazareth the commission that the Father had given to Him. He read from Isaiah 61:1 these words: *The Spirit of the Lord God is upon me; because the Lord hath anointed me to preach good tidings unto the meek; he hath sent me to bind up the broken hearted, to proclaim liberty to the captives, and the opening of the prison to them that are bound; to proclaim the acceptable year of the Lord.* The Lord reached this point in Isaiah 61:1, closed the book, returned it to the attendant and sat down. The eyes of all that were in the synagogue were fastened on Him, and He said unto them, *This day is this scripture fulfilled in your ears.*

In these verses, the Lord declared the acceptable year of the Lord. This was the beginning of the Gospel, the first element of the mystery of God. He was about to be completely denied, to be crucified, and to rise from the grave. After this, those who believe on Him would receive the Holy Spirit and the process of the mystery of God would begin. Later Paul would proclaim in 2 Corinthians 5:18-21 the continuance of the acceptable year of the Lord by declaring, *And all things are of God, who hath reconciled us to himself by Jesus Christ, and hath given to us the ministry of reconciliation; to wit, that God was in Christ, reconciling the world unto himself, not imputing their trespasses unto them; and hath committed unto us the word of reconciliation. Now then, we are ambassadors for Christ, as though God did beseech you by us: we pray you in Christ's stead, be ye reconciled to God. For he hath made him to be sin for us, who knew no sin; that we might be the righteousness of God in him.* 2 Corinthians 6:1-2 states, *We then, as workers together with him, beseech you also that ye receive not the grace of God in vain. For he saith, I have heard thee in a time accepted, and in the day of salvation have I succoured thee: behold, now is the day of salvation.* Paul made it clear that during our Lord's absence we are to continue in His stead to proclaim the acceptable year of the Lord. On the Isle of Patmos, the Lord gave to John the continuing commission of Isaiah 61:2, which was to declare the day of vengeance of our Lord.

Chapter 2

$\mathcal{The}$ Day of Vengeance

The verse in Revelation 10:11, unlike the commission expressed by Paul to all who are in the Church to declare the acceptable year of the Lord, is accomplished by only a part of the end-time Church. Our Lord addressed the Philadelphian Church with these words, *I know thy works: behold, I have set before thee an open door, and no man can shut it: for thou hast a little strength, and hast kept my word, and hast not denied my name* (Revelation 3:7-9). In the act of declaring the day of vengeance, the Philadelphians will express their love of the Savior, similar to the pure unselfish love that John expressed to Jesus when He faced the cross.

This love is manifested as it was expressed in Revelation 12:11, *And they overcame him [Satan] by the blood of the Lamb, and by the word of their testimony; and they loved not their lives unto the death.* This "word of their testimony" will be the "open door." It will be declaring the day of vengeance of our Lord.

Those participating in this commission will have knowledge. They will know that they will be completing the commission given to Jesus by the Father (Isaiah 61:2). They will know their testimony of judgment (when the power of the holy people is scattered) will fall on the ungodly (who have temporarily prevailed against God's purposes and His saints). They will declare Psalm 2:1-4, *Why do the heathen rage, and the people imagine a vain thing? The kings of the earth set themselves, and the rulers take counsel together, against the Lord, and against his anointed, saying, let us break their bands asunder, and cast their cords from us. He that sitteth in the heavens shall laugh: the Lord shall have them in derision.*

The Philadelphian Church will declare the day of reconciliation, that all the Church should be declaring, but in a more definite manner. They will be saying "Come, turn to Jesus now for the end of the age is here." Now is the time that the mystery of God will end, and the body of Christ will have its fulfillment. Now is the time while God's love is open to all who will come. This Church will declare the Day of Wrath with definite judgment to those outside of Christ. They will declare Psalm 1:5-6, *Therefore the ungodly shall not stand in the judgment, nor sinners in the congregation of the righteous. For the Lord knoweth the way of the righteous: but the way of the ungodly shall perish.* They will proclaim what will occur on the Resurrection-Wrath Day.

This declaration of judgment will be like flames of fire coming from their mouths. The very words of judgment consume their enemies who are in unbelief. The judgment might not be instantaneous, but it will eventually be fulfilled by including them in the completeness of God's word of judgment and wrath. Everyone surviving the Resurrection-Wrath Day will be subject to the Great Tribulation until the 1335th day of the 70th week. Survival will be the single goal for those who do not perish on this judgment day. The Lord will return the Philadelphian Church's testimony and love for Him. We read these words in Revelation 3:9, *Behold, I will make them of the synagogue of Satan, which say*

Chapter 2

they are Jews, and are not, but do lie; behold I will make them to come and worship before thy feet, and to know that I have loved thee.

Chapter 3

CHAPTER 3

EVENTS OF THE 70th WEEK

During the culminating events described in Chapter 2, God will once again begin dealing with the Jews as a nation. We, as the Church, will participate in the first 3-1/2 years of the 70th week. The Day of Grace, or the Church Age, will end on the Resurrection-Wrath Day. This will be the 1260th day of the 70th week; on this day, we are resurrected. Because of what occurred at our Lord's resurrection, we are able to participate in the first general resurrection and be taken out of God's wrath. Following is a brief sketch of the events that allows us to participate in this first general resurrection of the multitudes. MID TRIBULATION

At the cross Jesus was cut off, ending the 69th week of the 70 weeks given to the Jews to fulfill (Daniel 9:26). This was the day that He fulfilled the Law perfectly. Doing so gave Him the right to build His Church. Three days after the cross, He became the

Jesus Is Coming—A Different Perspective

fulfillment of the wave-sheaf offering in Leviticus 23. This was the first resurrection from the dead of those who were already asleep in God. Those already asleep in God are one of the wave-loaves offering at the resurrection. After His resurrection, all power was given unto Him. After this, is also when He, for forty days, appeared in His resurrected form and instructed the chosen apostles and disciples who believed on him, numbering about 120. Ten days after His ascension, on the Feast of Pentecost, He began to baptize believers with the Holy Spirit. This process brought into existence a new creation called saints or the holy people. This baptism makes each member of the Church eligible for resurrection. Our resurrection is the result of God (Jesus) doing everything.

The First Half of the 70th Week

All prophetic scripture has its center and core around the Israelites. It was to them that God gave the responsibility of preserving the written scriptures. It was from them the Messiah was to come. God works through them in their belief and unbelief to bring the knowledge of the one and true God to the world. It is only through the Israelites that we can understand our Christian position on God's timetable. This revealing timetable will bring to fulfillment a new heaven and a new earth. The 70th week is the last seven years of a 490-year program, which God has predestined the Jewish nation to fulfill. The program began when the commandment to restore the wall and build Jerusalem was given in Nehemiah 2; it was interrupted almost two thousand years ago when our Lord Jesus Christ was crucified (Daniel 9:26).

46

Chapter 3

This period (the 70th week) is the time in which God will end the "time of the Gentiles" and the "Day of Grace." Before our Lord comes for us, several things must occur to bring about this event. First is the scattering of the power of the holy people. Second, the Antichrist must be revealed. Third, the idol must be set up in the holy place. And fourth, the great falling away will occur. The events accomplishing the scattering of the power of the holy people are outlined in chapters 8, 9, and 10 of Revelation, which encompasses the seven trumpets. The last three and a half days before the Lord returns, the two witnesses will lie dead in the streets of Jerusalem. This will symbolically terminate the scattering of the power of the holy people. Indeed the day of our resurrection can be known by most of the Church before it happens. The Church will know that they will be raptured when the two witnesses rise or shortly thereafter. The Church will be raptured at the seventh trumpet when it begins to sound. God's wrath then will be initiated within hours after we rise as the seventh trumpet continues (Luke 17:29-30; Revelation 11:15). These trumpet events will bring the 70th week to its 1260th day.

The Trumpets

My attempt to give an interpretation of the trumpets is just that—an attempt. I do not believe these trumpets can be completely known until their completion is accomplished; however, God has given us enough so that we can be fairly accurate. God has decreed that the power of the holy people will be dispersed and that, eventually, His saints must be overcome by the Antichrist. The process of this will bring two definite results: (1) It will strengthen true believers, and (2) False professors of Christianity will be separated. God has also decreed that during this period the "Day of Vengeance" must be preached (Isaiah 61:2, Revelation 10:8-11, and 1 John 2:18-27).

Perhaps the hardest of the seven trumpets to interpret is the first trumpet. Revelation 8:7 states, *The first angel sounded, and there followed hail and fire mixed with blood, and they were cast upon the earth: and the third part of trees was burnt up, and all green grass was burnt up.* A paraphrase of this trumpet could be stated thus: The first trumpet is blown and God's two witnesses continue their last 3-1/2 year testimony concerning the Church and Israel. One-third of strong-in-the-Word believers will respond and participate in this testimony. All green grass (those who will respond and be saved) will receive this testimony before the Day of Wrath comes. Psalm 18:13 and Revelation 9:4 are two verses that are essential in interpreting this trumpet.

The second trumpet reads: *And the second angel sounded, and as it were a great mountain burning with fire was cast into the sea: and the third of the sea became blood; and the third part of the creatures which were in the sea, and had life, died; and the third part of the ships were destroyed* (Revelation 8:3-9). It is my belief that this trumpet will be accomplished in the Persian Gulf soon.

The third trumpet is a little different. My conclusions regarding it require further explanation,

Chapter 3

which I have included in the form of comments. Before beginning the explanation, it will be helpful to read the verses. *And the third angel sounded and there fell a great star from heaven, burning as though it was a lamp, and it fell upon the third part of the rivers and upon the fountains of waters. And the name of the star is called Wormwood: and the third part of the waters became wormwood; and many men died of the waters, because they were made bitter* (Revelation 8:10-11).

The Bible dictionary states that the word "star" is often used metaphorically in Scripture, usually to imply dignity, either innate or usurped. In our present verse, a star named Wormwood fell from heaven. The star was burning like a lamp giving light. This implies that this star brought forth what seemed to be great knowledge. This knowledge fell upon the third part of the rivers, or as I interpret it, a third part of individual believers; and upon the fountains of water or church denominations. That these rivers represent individual believers is demonstrated by our Lord's words in John 7:38, *He that believeth on me, as scripture hath said, out of his belly flows rivers of living water.* This trumpet is again described for us in Revelation 10:1-11. In verse 11, a commission was given to John. This commission is actually transferred to the believing end-time Church, which, like John, has a great love for the Savior. This testimony will be sweet in our mouths but bitter in our bellies. Please read John 21:21-23. The scattering of the power of the holy people will have been going on for some time. After the second trumpet, this process will accelerate. With the activities of the False Prophet, whom Satan will have indwelt, the great falling away mentioned in 2 Thessalonians 2:3-4 will occur. Even though the Antichrist overcomes the Church for a short period of time, the saints will overcome Satan by the blood of the Lamb and by the words of their testimony; and they loved not their lives unto the death (Revelation 12:11). Another way of saying this is they overcame Satan by blood, hail, and fire.

And the fourth angel sounded, and the third part of the sun was smitten, and the third part of the moon, and the third part of the stars: so that the third part of them was darkened, and the day shone not for a third part of it, and the night likewise.

Revelation 8:12

There are several passages in Scripture that refer directly to this verse. One is when our Lord said in Luke 21:25-26, *And there shall be signs in the sun, and in the moon, and in the stars; and upon the earth distress of nations, with perplexity; the sea and waves roaring; men's hearts failing them for fear, and for looking after those things which are coming on the earth: for the powers of heaven shall be shaken.* This fourth trumpet will be a great sign for the Church and a great testimony to the world. It is my belief that the above phenomenon occurs when God opens the third heaven and sends forth His angels to cleanse the heaven of this earth. Indeed the power of heaven shall be shaken, for this is the time during which Isaiah 34:5 will be accomplished, *For my sword shall be bathed in heaven: behold, it shall come down upon Idumea, and upon the people of my curse, to judgment.* It is interesting to note that this "sign" in heaven had a definite time span of eight hours. This fact brings to

Chapter 3

mind a second passage that deals specifically with this trumpet. Amos 8:9 states, *And it shall come to pass in that day, saith the Lord God, that I will cause the sun to go down at noon, and I will darken the earth in the clear day.* Of this day Joel states, *The sun shall be turned into darkness, and the moon into blood, before the great and the terrible day of the Lord come"*(Joel 2:31). He also states in Joel 3:15, *The sun and the moon shall be darkened, and the stars shall withdraw their shining.*

There are many who interpret this verse as referring to the Day of the Lord, which will occur at the seventh trumpet, especially since the next verse continues and states, *The Lord also shall roar out of Zion, and utter his voice from Jerusalem; and the heavens and the earth shall shake; but the Lord will be the hope of his people, and the strength of the children of Israel.* That Joel 3:15 is part of the fourth trumpet and not the seventh trumpet can readily be understood when comparing scripture with scripture.

Zechariah 14:6-7 gives the following description of the Day of the Lord, *And it shall come to pass in that day, that the light shall not be clear, nor dark: but it shall be one day which shall be known to the Lord, not day, nor night: but it shall come to pass, that at evening time, it shall be light.* The last reference to this trumpet occurs in Ezekiel 32:7-8. In these verses, God addresses Pharaoh (Satan) and states to him: *And when I shall put thee out, I will cover the heaven, and make the stars thereof dark; I will cover the sun with a cloud, and the moon shall not give her light. All the bright lights of heaven will I make dark over thee, and set darkness upon thy land, saith the Lord God.*

The last three trumpets, because of their effects on the human race, incorporate three woes. The fourth trumpet, which is Satan being cast from heaven to the earth, will bring about the first woe. The first woe occurs at the fifth trumpet when Satan is released from the abyss.

The sixth trumpet brings about the loosening of four angels who are prepared to destroy the third part of men, on an exact hour and day. After the loosening of the angels and the rising of the two witnesses but before the Church is raptured, a great earthquake will hit Jerusalem. A tenth of the city will fall and 7,000 will be killed, thus completing the second woe.

The third woe occurs at the seventh trumpet, after the Church is taken out. It is then that the wrath of God is dispensed. God's wrath and vengeance will be accomplished in a matter of hours. He will gather multitudes for a great sacrifice at Megiddo, located on the north side of the plains of Jezreel. Within hours after this carnage, He will bring great destruction upon the whole earth. He will do this by hailstones and a great earthquake that will result because of His shaking the heaven and earth. Isaiah 13:1-16 gives a vivid picture of God's wrath. Verses 9 through thirteen are quoted here to illustrate the severity it will have on mankind.

Verse 9: *Behold, the day of the Lord cometh, cruel both with wrath and fierce anger, to lay the land desolate: and he shall destroy the sinners thereof out of it.*

Verse 10: This verse refers to the fourth trumpet: *For the stars of heaven and the constellations thereof*

Chapter 3

shall not give their light: the sun shall be d
his going forth, and the moon shall not cause ner ught
to shine.

Verse 11: *And I will punish the world for their evil, and the wicked for their iniquity; and I will cause the arrogancy of the proud to cease, and will lay low the haughtiness of the terrible.*

Verse 12: *I will make a man more precious than fine gold; even a man than the golden wedge of Ophir.*

Verse 13: *Therefore I will shake the heavens, and the earth shall remove out of her place, in the wrath of the Lord of hosts, and in the day of his fierce anger.*

Please also read Jeremiah 25:29-38, noting especially verse 33, and Jeremiah 50:46.

The Bowls of Wrath

Since the three woes of the last three trumpets have a direct bearing on the bowls of wrath, we will address the bowls here. There are four controlling factors over the bowls of wrath. These factors are (1) Satan's work in the False Prophet, (2) the release of the four destroying angels, (3) the physical return of the Lord in judgment, and (4) God the Father's direct action (shaking of the heavens and the earth) when the Lord's feet touch down on the Mount of Olives. Following is a list of the seven bowls of wrath with brief comments about each. The reader should keep in mind that the sum of these bowls makes up the wrath of God.

1st Bowl: Foul and painful sores come upon the men who have the mark of the beast and upon them who have worshiped his image.

> *Comment:* Perhaps this is the result of the first woe when men are tormented for five months, possibly by nuclear fallout or poison gases.

2nd Bowl: The Mediterranean Sea becomes like the blood of a dead man, and every living soul in the sea dies.

> *Comment*: This is probably a result of God shaking the earth. Since the Mediterranean is confined by land all around it, it is likened to a dead man's blood. The sea will literally turn red from silt on the bottom of its floor. This has occurred on occasions in history when great earthquakes and volcanic action has taken place. These incidents will pale in comparison with events that will occur when God shakes the earth. Those on boats and in submarines will be killed. Much of the marine life will die and become a stench in the water.

3rd Bowl: The rivers and fountains of waters become blood.

> *Comment*: This is also a result of God shaking the earth.

4th Bowl: Men are scorched by the sun.

> *Comment*: Here again this will be caused by the earth being moved out of its place when God shakes the earth (Isaiah 13:13).

Chapter 3

5th Bowl: *The seat of the beast; and his kingdom was full of darkness; and they gnawed their tongues for pain* (Revelation 16:10).

> *Comment*: God brings darkness at the fourth trumpet. Pain is brought at the seventh trumpet when Satan's followers are placed into the Lake of Fire.

6th Bowl: The Euphrates was dried up so that the way of the kings of the East might be prepared.

> *Comment*: God dries up the Euphrates River so the way of the kings of the East is prepared, and He releases the destroying angels to bring about Armageddon. Satan does his part to bring about this bowl by sending lying spirits to gather the nations. Finally, the Lord's appearance will finish this bowl. THE 6th BOWL IS ARMAGEDDON.

7th Bowl: *...there was a great earthquake, such as was not since men were upon the earth...and the great city (Jerusalem) was divided into three parts, and the cities of the nations fell: And Great Babylon came in remembrance before God, to give unto her the cup of the wine of the fierceness of his wrath. And every island fled away, and the mountains were not found* (Revelation 16:18-20). *And there fell upon men a great hail out of heaven, every stone about the weight of a talent* (Revelation 16:20).

Comment: When God shakes the earth, the cities will crumble. Since the earth's surface is three-fourths water, the shaking will cause great tidal waves that will literally wash away the crumbled cities. Those cities that escape this will not escape the fires and crushing blows of the huge hailstones that follow.

When the earth is shaken, the heaven is also shaken. It will be then that *...the stars of heaven fell unto the earth, even as a fig tree casteth her untimely figs, when she is shaken of a mighty wind* (Revelation 6:13). These stars are the tares of Matthew 13, which have been gathered to be burned during the war in heaven. This war ends when Satan is cast to the earth at the 4th trumpet.

The Two Witnesses

In the first half of the 70th Week, God will be dealing with both Christians and Jews. To understand this, we must go back to Daniel 7:21-28. In these verses, the saints of the Most High (Christians) are witnesses for the Ancient of Days (Christ). These saints are also called the holy people in Daniel 12:7. When God established Israel as a nation, they were meant to be holy people, a position they never achieved as a nation. God always reserved to Himself a believing remnant, as He explained to Elias (Romans 11:3-4 and 1 Kings 19:18). In the fullness of time, God brought about Pentecost and created a holy people called saints of the Most High and, for the last two thousand years, Christians.

Chapter 3

The believing remnant from throughout the ages will become the people of the saints of the Most High, and they will be resurrected with Christians at the time our Lord's comes for us. The Millennial Kingdom will be given to the "people" of the saints of the Most High. This group will include the Jewish witnesses who come into being at the start of the 70th week 3-1/2 years before the completion of the Feast of Trumpets, the Resurrection-Wrath Day. After the Feast of Trumpets, the next feast that must be completed before the end of the 70th week is the Day of Atonement. It is then that God begins changing His people as a nation. With the beginning of the 70th week, a new Jewish witness begins, and these witnesses shall take their place as the people of the saints of the Most High. In Zechariah and Revelation both the Christians and the Jews are referred to as witnesses. They will be witnesses for God as He brings to a close the end of the age. The Jew will declare God's Word in *the spirit of Elijah.* Elijah was commissioned to *turn the heart of the fathers to the children, and the heart of the children to their fathers* (Malachi 4:6). In the same manner that John the Baptist was the precursor of Elijah when the Lord walked this earth (Matthew 11:14; Luke 1:17), this witness from the Jewish community will continue until the Lord's return in judgment. The Christian will declare God's Word in the spirit of the Apostle John. The fulfillment of Revelation 10:11 will be accomplished by Christians who declare *"the Day of Wrath"* or *"the day of vengeance",* which will be executed by their King of Kings and Lord of Lords.

The following scriptures and explanatory comments will illustrate to the reader the significance of the two witnesses' testimony.

Psalm 2:1-3: *Why do the heathen [nations] rage, and the people imagine a vain thing? The kings of the earth set themselves, and the rulers take counsel together, against the Lord, and against his anointed, saying, Let us break their bands asunder, and cast their cords from us.*

Revelation 11:9-10: *And they of the people and kindreds and tongues and nations shall see their dead bodies three days and an half, and shall not suffer their dead bodies to be put in graves. And they that dwell upon the earth shall rejoice over them, and make merry, and shall send gifts one to another; because these two prophets tormented them that dwelt on the earth.*

Comment: The witness of the Judeo-Christian religions gives a message that all mankind is accountable to God. We Christians are very verbal about everyone being a sinner with a tremendous need of a Savior. This message will continue to be rejected, and hostility toward all Christians and Jews will increase.

The world does not realize that the Lord considers the persecution of His Church as persecution of Him, for we are His body on earth.

Revelation 11:4: *These are the two olive trees, and the two candlesticks standing before the God of the earth.*

Chapter 3

Revelation 11:7: *And when they shall have finished their testimony, the beast that ascendeth out of the bottomless pit shall make war against them, and overcome them, and kill them.*

Comment: Through this act of Satan, God accomplishes Zechariah 11:7-14. In these verses, God deals with the two witnesses, here called Beauty and Bands. The Christian witness is called Beauty and the Jewish witness, Bands. God said He took his staff Beauty and *cut it asunder, that I might break my covenant which I had made with all the people* (Zechariah 11:10). *And it was broken in that day: and so the poor of the flock that waited upon me knew it was the word of the Lord* (Zechariah 11:11). Zechariah 11:14 continues and says, *"Then I cut asunder mine other staff, even Bands, that I might break the brotherhood between Judah and Israel."* From this point on the nation of Israel will be one in God. In a matter of hours, 144,000 Jews will be sealed to go through God's wrath. Great confidence and strength can be obtained from God's Word at this particular time, especially by reading Psalm 7 and 18, which reflect Joel 3:16. To me, Psalm 7 reflects the hope of Christians and Psalm 18, the strength of the children of Israel.

Revelation 11:5-7: *And if any man will hurt them, fire proceedeth out of their mouth, and devoureth their enemies; and if any man will hurt them, he must in this manner be killed. These have power to shut heaven, that it rain not in the days of their prophecy: and have power over waters to turn them to blood, and to smite the earth with all plagues, as often as they will.*

Comment: The very nature of the witnesses' prophecies condemns and sentences those who will hurt them. The message is one of God's judgment, and His word (fire) proceeding from their mouth is sure and definite. These two witnesses have power. I doubt that the Jewish witness will realize his position and power. The Christian witness is one of nonviolence, and he will proclaim God's Word of wrath without fear of retaliation. We read in Romans 12:17-21, *Recompense to no man evil for evil. Provide things honest in the sight of all men. If it be possible, as much as lieth in you, live peaceably with all men. Dearly beloved, avenge not yourselves, but rather give place unto wrath: for it is written, Vengeance is mine; I will repay, saith the Lord. Therefore if thine enemy hunger, feed him; if he thirst, give him to drink: for in so doing thou shalt, heap coals of fire on his head. Be not overcome of evil, but overcome evil with good.*

At the Lord's return, He comes in judgment of unregenerate man and causes His Jewish nation to be gathered and refined. Our Lord re-ascends with His saints to His heavenly kingdom. During and at the Lord's return, two-thirds of the population of Israel will die. The one-third Jewish survivors will be refined and tested. They eventually call upon Jesus as Lord (Zechariah 13:8-9). Do not be confused as this reigning of the Lord is not the idyllically described millennial reign. The 70th week has not yet been completed, and God's covenants with and prophecies regarding His people must be fulfilled (Acts 3: 19-21). This is the purpose of the 70 weeks. When the Lord died on

Chapter 3

the cross, He had accomplished most of the objectives of the 70 weeks. He had made it possible to make an end of sins, to make reconciliation for iniquities, and to bring in everlasting righteousness. The Jewish nation rejected Him at His first coming, however, and the 70th week was postponed until the "end of the age." The remaining requirements of the first half of the 70th week are accomplished by the two witnesses. In the latter half of the 70th week, God will end the transgression of His people by gathering them and changing them as a nation. He will seal up the vision and prophecy by fulfilling all visions and prophecies concerning the Jewish nation prior to the millennial age. The anointing of the most Holy will be accomplished after the Jewish priests cleanse the sanctuary. When all these things have been accomplished, the 70th week will end. The Lord Jesus will see that all these things are accomplished. In Isaiah 61:1-3 we read our Lord's commission. Following are these three verses with comments for clarification.

Isaiah 61:1: *The Spirit of the Lord God is upon me; because the Lord hath anointed me to preach good tidings unto the meek; he hath sent me to bind up the brokenhearted, to proclaim liberty to the captives, and the opening of the prison to them that are bound.*

Comment: As mentioned above the Lord literally accomplished all these things during His three and a half year ministry on earth. His ministry ended the 69th week.

Isaiah 61:2: *To proclaim the acceptable year of the Lord, and the day of vengeance of our God; to comfort all that mourn.*

Comment: Our Lord proclaimed the acceptable year of the Lord and then commissioned His Church to carry on this responsibility during His absence. For nearly two thousand years, the true Church has been a witness to and has proclaimed that today is the day of salvation. Paul said it so clearly in

2 Corinthians 6:1-2: *We then, as workers together with him, beseech you also that ye receive not the grace of God in vain. For he saith, I have heard thee in a time accepted, and in a day of salvation have I succoured [helped] thee; behold now is the accepted time; behold, now is the day of salvation.*

Our Lord did not proclaim the day of vengeance during His earthly ministry. When He read these verses from Isaiah in the synagogue at Nazareth (Luke 4:16-21), He stopped with the words "year of the Lord." Who then will proclaim, "The day of vengeance of our God?" It is my belief that many of those Christians who are to be raptured will proclaim the day of vengeance. The last phrase of this verse states, "to comfort all that mourn." All Christians who mourn prior to our Lord's return in judgment are comforted by the fact of His promised return for them before He executes His wrath. For a short time, the devout Jew will be under the thumb of Antichrist. These Jews will know from God's Word what the outcome of their position will

Chapter 3

be. They will be comforted by many scriptures that show their deliverance and the eventual return of their Messiah to reign.

Isaiah 61:3: *To appoint unto them who mourn in Zion,* (the regathering process) *to give unto them beauty for ashes, the oil of joy for mourning, the garment of praise for the spirit of heaviness; that they might be called trees of righteousness, the planting of the Lord, that he might be glorified.*

Comment: These things will occur after the "glory," after the day of vengeance. The spirit of Elijah dominates the Jewish witnesses until the Day of Wrath. The Lord then takes over and converts all that are gathered. Read Zechariah 2 and 3. Zechariah 3 is a beautiful picture of Israel being reinstated into her priestly office as a nation. It is when the Lord takes away Israel's self-righteousness and causes her to seek after God's righteousness that they will be called trees of righteousness.

During the latter half of the 70th week, Satan is still allowed to be active in many of the nations. He will persecute the Jewish remnant, and they will flee to the wilderness of Israel (Isaiah 64:19-21; Zechariah 10:9-12; Jeremiah 30:2; Hosea 2:14). God, in various ways, will cause the remaining Jewish remnant to return to Israel (Deuteronomy 30:3; Isaiah 66:19-21; Jeremiah 30:10-17). The remnant will find themselves in a land that is a devastated wilderness. The Israelites that survived the Lord's appearance will be there when the remnant arrives. They will instruct the remnant of the need for repenting and turning completely to God. This is the same message started by John the Baptist. This is the same message the Israelites will have heard from the two witnesses. The survivors living in Israel will also assure the returning Israelites of their safety, since all Israelites are divinely protected by the Lord. This new but not completely converted Israel will dwell in safely in the land until just prior to the sanctuary being cleansed (Daniel 8:14). Satan, having been frustrated in his attempts to persecute the Jewish remnant, will make an attempt to eradicate the new Israel by bringing Gog and Magog against her, but he will be thwarted in his attempt (Ezekiel 38 and 39, noting especially 39:12). This is similar to but not the same as the Gog-Magog battle recorded in Revelation 20:8-9. The sanctuary is cleansed and salvation comes to Israel. The Palestinian Covenant ceases (Deuteronomy 30:1-10), and Israel repents and turns completely to God. Satan is cast into the pit and sealed for a thousand years. The Lord returns to reign on Mount Zion. A new, everlasting covenant is made (Ezekiel 16:60-63; Ezekiel 37:26; Jeremiah 31:33).

The Resurrection-Wrath Day

In the book of Daniel Chapter 12, "the end" is repeated several times. The end of all the events in Chapter 11 and the resurrection and the scattering of the power of the holy people (Christians) in this chapter will occur during the first half of the 70th week. This illustrates the fact that we Christians will

Chapter 3

be here after God begins dealing with the Jewish nation once again. The end of the age will culminate on the 1260th day of the 70th week. We Christians have been promised by the Savior that He would be with us unto the end of the age (Matthew 28:20).

As discussed previously, the book of Revelation gives the end-time Christians seals and trumpets to guide them through this period, which will culminate with the Resurrection-Wrath Day (also referred to as the Day of the Lord and the end of the age). Paul informed believers that the idol would be put up and the great falling away, which is our Lord separating out the apostate church, would occur so that day would not catch them unawares.

Paul on Mars Hill in Acts 17:31 states that God has appointed a day in which His wrath would be poured out on the ungodly. In Daniel chapters 8 and 11, an angel declares several times that that day would occur on the appointed day. The last appointed day occurred at Pentecost with the creation of the holy people, Christians. The next appointed day will be the Resurrection-Wrath Day (the Day of the Lord), which will fulfill The Feast of Trumpets. This day will occur on the 1260th day of the 70th week. The Feast of Passover will occur 1260 days later, completing the 70th week. The Feast of Trumpets is always celebrated on the first day of Tishri, the seventh month on the Jewish calendar.

Our Lord's parable of the master traveling into a far country and leaving talents to his servants to invest while he is gone (Matthew 25:14-30) demonstrates the Church Age and the ending of the age. The tares among the wheat parable in Matthew 13:24-30 and 24:37-43 shows how we Christians will be here with false believers until the end of the age. Revelation 10:7 is a description of the resurrection day, the day the mystery of God is completed, which occurs when the seventh angel begins to sound the trumpet. This day is followed by God's wrath, which occurs while the sound of the seventh angel's trumpet continues. These conditions are described for us in Revelation 11:18, *And the nations were angry, and thy wrath is come, and the time of the dead, that they should be judged, and that thou shouldest give reward unto thy servants the prophets, and to the saints and them that fear thy name, small and great; and shouldest destroy them which destroy the earth.* In this one verse, we have described for us the Resurrection-Wrath Day.

Our Lord's testimony in Luke 17:28-37 is more specific in revealing that the Day of Wrath, the appointed day, is the same day as the resurrection day. In verses 29 and 30 of this chapter, He said, *But the same day that Lot went out of Sodom it rained fire and brimstone from heaven, and destroyed them all. Even thus shall it be in the day when the Son of man is revealed.* The verses that follow this declaration describe those who are raptured and those who are left behind. The children of Israel are among those left behind. These are the ones who will depend on the strength of the Lord to be delivered (Joel 3:16) and will include the 144,000 sealed Jews (Revelation 7:4). Two more groups remain: Those who will be damned, and those who will survive this Day of Wrath and reach the

Chapter 3

1335th day of the 70th week. The survivors will eventually enter into the millennial reign of Christ. From the above scriptures, one can readily see that the Day of the Lord, (the Resurrection-Wrath Day,) brings an end to the time of the Gentiles and to the time of the end of the age. These terms are simply referring to the end of the dispensation of grace, the Church Age. God's program will continue until the completion of the 70th week and the fulfillment of the remaining feasts of the Lord.

CHAPTER 4

THE END TIMES

Resources for the Church

When Jesus started building His Church, He did not leave it without resources to see each generation victoriously to its end. Following is a list of some of these resources, which we are able to use to accomplish victory:

1. The Church has been given His righteousness.

2. The Church has been given His peace.

3. The Church has been given His promises.

4. The Church was given the New Testament.

5. The Church was given the Holy Spirit to teach each generation the things that were needed for that generation.

6. The Church has been given additional information pertaining to Old Testament prophecies through the New Testament.

The end-time Church, through Jesus' testimony, can know the time of their resurrection by:

- combining Leviticus 23 with the book of Revelation
- understanding the 70th week through the study of the New Testament writings
- gaining a clear understanding of the three resurrections

It is hopeful that this chapter will bring hard-to-understand scriptures together in their proper timing and meaning.

Troubling Verses for the Church

The Mystery of God

But in the days of the voice of the seventh angel, when he shall begin to sound, the mystery of God should be finished, as he hath declared to his servants the prophets.

Revelation 10:7

The mystery of God is tied up with the beginning and the ending of the dispensation of grace. The Church began with Pentecost, and it will end with the completion of the Feast of Trumpets. This mystery is

Chapter 4

revealed to us in the book of Ephesians and in 1 Peter 1:9-13. It was Paul who described the depth of the dispensation of grace, though it is not the "mystery" that is finished at the seventh trumpet; even though the dispensation will also be concluded at that time.

In 1 Peter 1:9-13 we have been given the information to figure out the mystery of God. 1 Peter 1:10 is one of the key verses that begins to reveal the mystery. It states, *Of which salvation the prophets have enquired and searched diligently, who prophesied of the grace that should come unto you.* The prophets did not know what the dispensation of grace would entail. They did not know any detail that would distinguish this grace, which was to come to both Jews and Gentiles. They only knew that it would eventually occur. They could search for the details and meaning of this grace but to no avail.

In Ephesians 3:2, Paul says that the dispensation of the grace of God was given to him. Even though past scriptures revealed there would be a great salvation movement for all on the earth, it was given to Paul to explain it to the Gentiles, who knew nothing about Judaism, the Mosaic Law, etc. In Ephesians 3:5 he said it was not made known in other ages. Peter declared that the prophets knew and prophesied the grace that would come to Christians. What was it, then, that was not made known in other ages? What is the mystery "hidden in God"? When God made declarations in past scriptures, He did not reveal the scope of the dispensation of grace. That was left to Paul and other Christians who would build upon His work. God did, however, make definite revelations in past scriptures, and it was given to Paul to bring three keys to understanding the dispensation of grace and the mystery of the dispensation of grace.

What is the mystery? What was it that the prophets of old did not understand? They did not know (1) the "gospel," the person of Jesus and His ministry, (2) the power of the Holy Spirit that He would give to those who believed on Him, and (3) the effectiveness of the believers using that power to reach others. For two thousand years, this process has been going on. It is the mystery hidden in God, and it is the greatest evangelistic program used to bring multitudes into the Kingdom of God. This is the mystery of God that will be finished when the seventh trumpet begins to sound.

God indicated this mystery (the evangelistic process) with a statement He declared in Leviticus 23:22, *And when ye reap the harvest of your land, thou shalt not make clean riddance of the corners of thy field when thou reapest, neither shalt thou gather any gleaning of thy harvest: thou shalt leave them unto the poor, and to the stranger: I am the Lord your God.* Why did God make this statement after describing the progression of Pentecost and the two wave-loaves offering before describing the next feast, the Feast of Trumpets? What is the relevance of this declaration? Perhaps the Jew of that day thought it was just a reminder of God's declaration in Leviticus 19:9. This declaration certainly distinguished them from their surrounding heathen nations. This verse, to those of us on this side of Pentecost, draws us unashamedly to the book of Ruth. In this book, we get a picture of our kinsman redeemer and the bride of Christ. Scofield's introduction to this book states the Christian experience in terms of Ruth—deciding to serve Christ, serving Christ, resting in Christ, and being rewarded by Christ. In my interpretation, this reward is being one of the wave loaves at the resurrection.

The Covenant: Daniel 9:27

And he shall confirm a covenant with many for one week; and in the midst of the week he shall cause the sacrifice and the oblation to cease, and for the overspreading of abominations he shall make it desolate, even until the consummation, and that determined shall be poured upon the desolate.

Following is this same verse, with clarifications added:

And he (the False Prophet, Satan indwelling him) *shall confirm* (make solid) *a covenant made by the Antichrist. The covenant was for one week or seven years. And in the midst of the week almost 3-1/2 years, he* (the False Prophet indwelt by Satan) *shall cause the sacrifice and the oblation to cease,* (shall cause sacrifice of confession in prayer of the nation and the individual with thanksgiving to cease) *and for the overspreading of abominations* (and because of the seriousness of the abomination, setting up an idol in the holy place) *he shall make it* (a synagogue in Judah, its host), *desolate, even until the consummation,* (the end of the age), *and that determined shall be poured upon the desolate.*

The **Covenant: Psalm 83:3-8**

When: Approximately 3-1/2 years before the Resurrection-Wrath Day

What: *They have taken crafty counsel against thy people, and consulted against thy hidden ones.* ("Thy people" refers to Israel; "thy hidden" ones to Christians.)

Who: *They have said, Come, and let us cut them off from being a nation; that the name of Israel may be no more in remembrance. For they have consulted together with one consent; they are confederate against thee: the tabernacles of Edom, the Ishmaelites; of Moab, and the Hagarenes; Gebal, and Ammon, and Amalak; the Philistines with the inhabitants of Tyre; Assur also is joined with them: they have holpen the children of Lot.*

Comment: I have seen this confederation on T.V. several times in the past. The deceased King Hussian of Jordan was instrumental in bringing these Arab leaders together for many years. At first, only a handful of this confederation gathered. Through time, their gathering has become more solid. I was impressed with this gathering at the occasion of King Hussian funeral in February 1999. It may have been at this time that the covenant to get rid of Israel was made. When the False Prophet appears, being indwelt by Satan, he will confirm this covenant. Please read Revelation 12:13-17.

Chapter 4

No Man Knows: Matthew 24:36

But of that day and hour knoweth no man, no, not the angels of heaven, but my Father only.

These three words, "no man knows", are as true today as when our Lord spoke them approximately two thousand years ago. It was a confirmation of what Paul would later declare in 1 Corinthians 2. When our Lord uttered these words, He stated them in the present tense. The cross was a few days off, and His resurrection would soon follow. Fifty days after His resurrection, at Pentecost, He began a new program for mankind (Isaiah 42:6). This new program made it possible for the person who put their faith in Jesus Christ, and was thereby born again, to become a new creation (Isaiah 42:8-9; 2 Corinthians 5:17). This new creation was a person with the Holy Spirit dwelling within. These people are called saints, the holy people, Christians. With this new creation, God would share His glory. He would give the New Testament to guide and empower them to seek out truth throughout the whole Bible. This seeking would allow the holy people to know the truth and the "when" of His return for them.

The Raptured Church: Revelation 7:9-17

There are many in the Church, probably most, who believe the Church is raptured in Chapter four of Revelation when John is commanded to "come up here." They will state that the word "church" is not mentioned from that point on in Revelation; however, John sees and describes the raptured church in Revelation 7: 9-17. What John sees are those who are taken out of Great Tribulation at the sixth seal or the seventh trumpet. These are part of the loaves offering. Where are the remaining parts of the two loaves at this particular time? How do I know that these are the raptured Church? The text itself says that they are taken out of the Great Tribulation. This of necessity must be part of those who are Christ's at His coming. There are only three resurrections: (1) the Lord's (the First Fruits feast), (2) those who are His at His coming, and (3) after the millennial reign of the Lord. There are no other resurrections, and there are no "so called" Tribulation saints—those saved after the resurrection of the Church. The Great Tribulation begins 30 days before the second resurrection and will end seventy-five days after the resurrection. This is revealed in Daniel 12. Those who survive the Great Tribulation period will be blessed to enter the millennial reign of the Lord. They could be part of the saved at the third resurrection.

The Great Falling Away

The Declaration: 2 Thessalonians 2:3

Let no man deceive you by any means: for that day shall not come, except there come a falling away first, and that man of sin be revealed, the son of perdition.

Chapter 4

The Third Trumpet: Revelation 8:10-11

And the third angel sounded, and there fell a great star from heaven, burning as it were a lamp, and it fell upon the third part of the rivers, and upon the fountains of waters; And the name of the star is called Wormwood: and the third part of the waters became wormwood; and many men died of the waters, because they were made bitter.

Message to the Church at Thyatira: Revelation 2:18-29

And unto the angel of the church in Thyatira write; These things saith the Son of God, who hath his eyes like unto a flame of fire, and his feet are like fine brass; I know thy works, and charity, and service, and faith, and thy patience, and thy works; and the last to be more than the first. Notwithstanding I have a few things against thee, because thou sufferest that woman Jezebel, which calleth herself a prophetess, to teach and to seduce my servants to commit fornication, and to eat things sacrificed unto idols. And I gave her space to repent of her fornication; and she repented not. Behold, I will cast her into a bed, and them that commit adultery with her into great tribulation, except they repent of their deeds. And I will kill her children with death; and all the churches shall know that I am he which searcheth the reins and hearts: and I will give unto every one of you according to your works. But unto you I say, and unto the rest in Thyatira, as many as have not this doctrine, and which have not known the depths of Satan, as they speak; I will put upon you none other burden. But that which ye have already hold fast till I come. And he that overcometh, and keepeth my works unto the end, to him will I give power over the nations: And he shall rule them with a rod of iron; as the vessels of a potter shall they be broken to shivers: even as I received of my Father. And I will give him the morning star. He that hath an ear, let him hear what the Spirit saith unto the churches.

Comment: Paul declares clearly that our Lord will not return for His Church until two things have been accomplished: (1) the great falling away from the Church and (2) the Antichrist is revealed. These two things will be accomplished at the end of the first half of the 70th week; thus, the Church will be here during the beginning of the first half of the 70th week. All the Church on earth will enter the Great Tribulation 30 days before they are raptured. During this period of 30 days, no one will be allowed to buy or sell without the seal of the Antichrist. When the idol of the Antichrist is set up in the holy place, there will be no doubt as to who he is. During this 30-day period, there will be ample time for professing Christians who have fornicated with that woman Jezebel, whom our Lord describes in His letter to Thyatira, to repent. When they repent, they must be overcomers, meaning they must know and declare that Jesus is the Son of God (1 John 5:1-5) and keep His word or commandment to the end. The end is until the end of the age, which culminates with the rapture. It is gratifying to know that only one-third of professing

Chapter 4

Christianity will go farther into the Great Tribulation period. They will be damned along with Jezebel, the False Prophet, and the Antichrist. The fifth chapter of Proverbs, which follows, and many others throughout all the scriptures, warns professing believers of being seduced by a Jezebel.

My son, attend unto my wisdom, and bow thine ear to my understanding: That thou mayest regard discretion, and that thy lips may keep knowledge. For the lips of a strange woman drop as an honeycomb, and her mouth is smoother than oil: But her end is bitter as wormwood, sharp as a two-edged sword. Her feet go down to death; her steps take hold of hell. Lest thou shouldest ponder the path of life, her ways are moveable, that thou canst not know them. Hear me now therefore, O ye children, and depart not from the words of my mouth. Remove thy way far from her, and come not nigh the door of her house: Lest thou give thine honour unto others, and thy years unto the cruel: Lest strangers be filled with thy wealth; and thy labours be in the house of a stranger; And thou mourn at the last, when thy flesh and thy body are consumed, And say, How have I hated instruction, and my heart despised reproof; And have not obeyed the voice of my teachers, nor inclined mine ear to them that instructed me! I was almost in all evil in the midst of the congregation and assembly. Drink waters out of thine own cistern, and running waters out of thine own well. Let thy fountains be dispersed abroad, and rivers of waters in the streets. Let them be only thine own, and not strangers' with thee. Let thy fountain be blessed: and rejoice with the wife of thy youth. Let her be as the loving hind and pleasant roe; let her breasts satisfy thee at all times;

and be thou ravished always with her love. And why wilt thou, my son, be ravished with a strange woman, and embrace the bosom of a stranger? For the ways of man are before the eyes of the Lord, and he pondereth all his goings. His own iniquities shall take the wicked himself, and he shall be holden with the cords of his sins. He shall die without instruction; and in the greatness of his folly he shall go astray.

Two Doctrines

Dear Reader,

We are the end-time Church. We have responsibilities that preceding Church members did not have. We must be more discerning about doctrines. Following are two doctrines that are examples of our need to be more definite in our understanding. The first given is "The Imminent Return of Christ." Most expositors will cling to the "any moment" return of Christ. The second is entitled "Resurrections." These doctrines, in most cases, lack enough information to be more definite.

The Imminent Return of Christ: A False Church Doctrine

I believe the scriptures teach that those in the Church are to live their lives as if the Lord would come at anytime. This was particularly important for the beginning Church and throughout the ages. Today, we are a part of the end-of-the-age Church, and we are to

Chapter 4

know when He is coming for us. Many events must occur before the Church is raptured. We know that the Antichrist will be destroyed with the brightness of the Lord's coming (2 Thessalonians 2:8) on the Resurrection-Wrath Day, the 1260th day of the 70th week. We know from Paul's writings that day will not occur until two events occur: the idol is placed in the temple and the great falling away occurs. These two events must occur before we are raptured. When referring to the location where the Antichrist will place the idol, Paul used the word temple, but our Lord used the words holy place. Since there is no temple today, and the temple will not be rebuilt until after our resurrection (Acts 15:13-18), where is the holy place our Lord referred to? I believe it is the synagogue of Hebron, where the patriarchs are buried. Even if the temple was rebuilt and the Antichrist put an idol up in it, it would not be a holy place. The temple is made holy on the last day of the 70th week when God anoints it. The idol is placed in the holy place 30 days before the resurrection. At the resurrection, the Church, the temple of God (Ephesians 2:19-22), is offered up to God the Father as one of the wave-loaves offerings (Leviticus 23:15-22). At this point, God has been dealing with Israel as a nation for 3-1/2 years. During this time, God is still building His living temple, the Church. A Jewish temple could be built in this 3-1/2 year period, but as I pointed out earlier, it will not be made holy until the last day of the 70th week. The Lord said the idol would be put up in a holy place. Paul could have used the word temple in his letter to the Thessalonians because they probably had knowledge of a time in Israel's history when this occurred. This

81

would have given them understanding that they could readily receive. In other words, Paul was using the word temple as a metaphor for a holy place. This is frequently done in scriptures. The second event that must occur, the great falling away, should be connected to the Laodicean Church, which the Lord spews out of his mouth because they were neither hot nor cold (see Revelation 3:14-16).

Paul states that the Church will be raptured at the last trumpet in 1 Corinthians 15:52 and at the sound of the trumpet in 1 Thessalonians 4:16. John lists the trumpets in Revelation. The six trumpets will occur before we are raptured at the last trumpet. I doubt that Paul knew that John would be listing them.

The scope of end-time studies illustrates the ending of the age. This is especially true in the book of Daniel. The angel interpreting to Daniel specifically states in Daniel 8:17, *O son of man: for at the time of the end shall be the vision* and in Daniel 10:14, *Now I am come to make thee understand what shall befall thy people in the latter days: for yet the vision is for many days.* The angel then continues describing events that must occur at the end of the age and, in Chapter 12, the resurrection. The Lord told the Church in Matthew 28:20, *Lo, I am with you always, even unto the end of the age.* How could we be taken out at any moment when the end of the age has not come? The end of the age is a day appointed in wrath; it is also the resurrection day. It is a day described by our Lord in Luke 17:29-30, *But the same day that Lot went out of Sodom it rained fire and brimstone from heaven, and destroyed them all. Even thus shall it be in the day*

Chapter 4

when the Son of man is revealed. This will occur on the first day of the seventh month on the Jewish calendar, on the Jewish Feast of Trumpets.

One can readily see that the Lord will not come at just anytime. He will not come for His Church until the end of the age comes. He will not come until the idol is set up in the holy place. He will not come until the power of the holy people is scattered (Daniel 12:7). He will not come until He has spewed the Laodicean Church out of His mouth. He will not come until all six trumpets that precede the seventh trumpet have occurred.

Because of these facts, it is my position that the Lord's imminent return for His Church is a false Church doctrine. I believe many denominations seem to embrace this false doctrine.

Resurrections

The first coming of Christ to the earth was as a baby. The second coming of Christ to the earth will be to gather His Church, the body of Christ. At this same time, the resurrection will occur. This resurrection will include those who are His, both Old Testament believers and His body, the Church. Our Lord's resurrection was the first resurrection of all those who were believers before Pentecost and the first of those who are indwelt by the Holy Spirit, the saints. These saints are deceased and are awaiting this resurrection in heaven. Prophetically, our Lord's resurrection is the wave sheaf offering, which fulfills the First Fruits

Feast (Leviticus 23:10-11; 1 Corinthians 15:23). This resurrection that occurs at His coming is the first general resurrection of mankind. None has ever preceded this resurrection. Those participating in this resurrection are called blessed, and the second death has no power over them. A second resurrection of the masses occurs one thousand years later, after the millennial reign of Christ over the earth.

When our Lord returns to this earth to pick up His Church, all the dead in Christ rise first, and those who remain (those believers alive on the earth) rise to meet them in the air. There are no believers in Christ, no other church, left behind. The whole body of Christ is taken at this time. There are no "so called" tribulation saints or Jewish church left behind. All who are in Christ, all who are His, are raptured and resurrected at this time. When this happens, all of mankind will see the glory of the Lord, as His glory will flash across the skies. Some unbelievers will immediately hide themselves in the dens of the earth, trying to escape from the wrath of the Lamb, wrath that will come upon all mankind that very day. This process, when the Church is raptured and the wrath of God is dispensed at the seventh trumpet, is described in Luke 17:29-30 and again in Revelation 11:15-19. When this resurrection occurs, it occurs on the 1260th day of the 70th week (Daniel 12). God begins dealing with the Jews as a nation 3-1/2 years before our resurrection. When the Jews rejected our Lord and had Him crucified, the Lord and the Jews were under the dispensation of law. While under law, they were given 70 weeks of years (490 years) to reach fulfillment. When the Lord was crucified, they had completed the

Chapter 4

69th week. When God again starts dealing with them as a nation, He will do so under the law. They must complete the 70th week under the dispensation of law. The Jews, during this present dispensation of grace, are given the same condition of entering the church as the entire world. They, as anyone else, must believe on Jesus to be born again. Three and a half years before this dispensation of grace comes to a close, the 70th week begins. This dispensation of grace ends on the Jewish Feast of Trumpets, leaving the Jews 3-1/2 years to the end of the 70th week.

The third resurrection (counting the Lord's) will be brought to pass approximately one thousand years after the first general resurrection. During this period, God makes a covenant of peace with Israel. This peace will be produced by Israel when the Spirit of God is poured upon them. Their righteous works that follow this outpouring of the Holy Spirit brings glory to God. What are these righteous works that will be accomplished by Israel? During the thousand-year reign of Christ, the nations of the world are commanded to keep the Feast of Tabernacles. They must go to Jerusalem to seek out the Lord their God. This is a forced law that must be kept (Zechariah 14:17-18). When representatives of the nations come to the temple, they will observe a cloud over it by day and a pillar of fire at night. They will observe the sacrificial offerings given under the law. It is my opinion that it is then that the righteous works of Israel will go into operation. Today, we who have the Holy Spirit in us proclaim the acceptable year of the Lord for salvation. In like manner, the Israelites will point the nations to Jesus and their opportunity for salvation through the grace of God to enter His kingdom. They will point out to the nations Israel's history and how God delivered them as a nation to salvation through Jesus Christ (Isaiah 61:3). This message will bring peace, quietness, and assurance to them as a nation. Multitudes will enter into the kingdom of God.

When this last resurrection occurs, it will differ from the second resurrection. At this time both believing mankind and unbelieving mankind are resurrected—believing mankind unto life, and the unbelieving unto damnation. The damned will be forced to bow before Jesus and to confess Him as Lord unto the glory of God the Father. The second death follows when God the Father calls back to Himself the spirit of life that He has given all mankind born of a woman. The souls of these unbelievers are then cast into the lake of fire.

Chapter 4

A Sample Time Line for End-Time Events

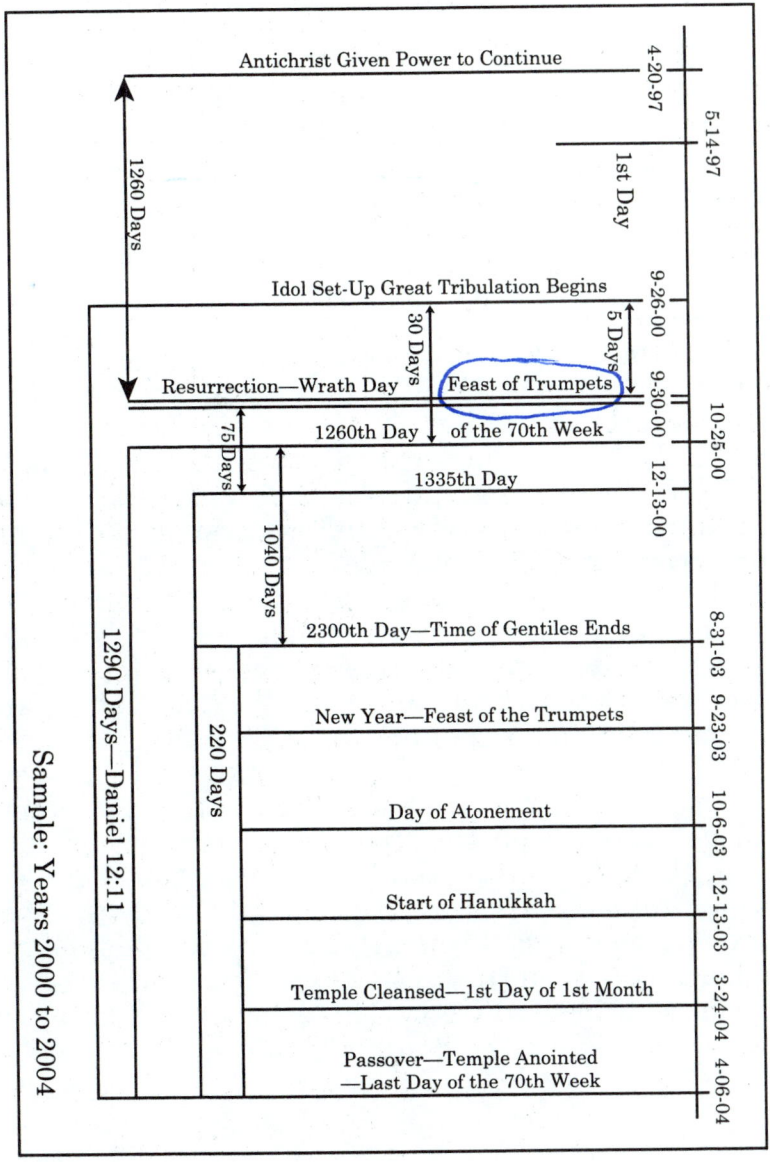

- Antichrist Given Power to Continue — 4-20-97
- 5-14-97 — 1st Day
- 1260 Days
- Idol Set-Up Great Tribulation Begins — 9-26-00
- 30 Days
- 5 Days
- Resurrection—Wrath Day | Feast of Trumpets — 9-30-00
- 1260th Day — of the 70th Week
- 10-25-00
- 75 Days
- 1335th Day — 12-13-00
- 1040 Days
- 2300th Day—Time of Gentiles Ends — 8-31-03
- New Year—Feast of the Trumpets — 9-23-03
- 220 Days
- Day of Atonement — 10-6-03
- Start of Hanukkah — 12-13-03
- Temple Cleansed—1st Day of 1st Month — 3-24-04
- Passover—Temple Anointed —Last Day of the 70th Week — 4-06-04

1290 Days—Daniel 12:11

Sample: Years 2000 to 2004

87

About This Time Line

This time line illustrates how the end-time Church can know, 3-1/2 years before it happens, when the Resurrection-Wrath Day will occur. Every year we can go to the Jewish Feast of Trumpets, which will generally occur in September or early October on our calendar. From that day, count forward 1260 days. When the 1260th day falls on the Passover Feast, you will have the year and day of the rapture.

This time line gives the timing for the Gog-Magog war described in Ezekiel 38 and 39 and discussed in Chapter 3 of this book. This war will occur on the 2300th day of the 70th week (Daniel 8:13-14). These verses cover the activities of the Antichrist at the beginning of the 70th week and his destruction at our Lord's coming. It also includes the 1040-day period in which the Jewish people are re-gathered to Israel and the period in which the new temple is built. The new temple is built after our Lord's return for us (Acts 15:13-18). Both the sanctuary and the host (Israel) are to be trodden underfoot until the 2300th day. After the Gog-Magog war, Israel will cleanse the land for seven months or 210 days (Ezekiel 39:12). The new temple will be cleansed on the first day of the first month (Ezekiel 45:18). After the cleansing of the land, the people will have ten days to cleanse themselves so the Lord will be glorified when He anoints the temple and makes it holy with His presence on the Passover Feast. All these things will occur in their proper assigned times according to the Word of God.

Chapter 4

2000

	JANUARY					
S	M	T	W	T	F	S
						1
2	3	4	5	6	7	8
9	10	11	12	13	14	15
16	17	18	19	20	21	22
23	24	25	26	27	28	29
30	31					

	FEBRUARY					
S	M	T	W	T	F	S
		1	2	3	4	5
6	7	8	9	10	11	12
13	14	15	16	17	18	19
20	21	22	23	24	25	26
27	28	29				

	MARCH					
S	M	T	W	T	F	S
			1	2	3	4
5	6	7	8	9	10	11
12	13	14	15	16	17	18
19	20	21	22	23	24	25
26	27	28	29	30	31	

	APRIL					
S	M	T	W	T	F	S
						1
2	3	4	5	6	7	8
9	10	11	12	13	14	15
16	17	18	19	20	21	22
23	24	25	26	27	28	29
30						

	MAY					
S	M	T	W	T	F	S
	1	2	3	4	5	6
7	8	9	10	11	12	13
14	15	16	17	18	19	20
21	22	23	24	25	26	27
28	29	30	31			

	JUNE					
S	M	T	W	T	F	S
				1	2	3
4	5	6	7	8	9	10
11	12	13	14	15	16	17
18	19	20	21	22	23	24
25	26	27	28	29	30	

	JULY					
S	M	T	W	T	F	S
						1
2	3	4	5	6	7	8
9	10	11	12	13	14	15
16	17	18	19	20	21	22
23	24	25	26	27	28	29
30	31					

	AUGUST					
S	M	T	W	T	F	S
		1	2	3	4	5
6	7	8	9	10	11	12
13	14	15	16	17	18	19
20	21	22	23	24	25	26
27	28	29	30	31		

	SEPTEMBER					
S	M	T	W	T	F	S
					1	2
3	4	5	6	7	8	9
10	11	12	13	14	15	16
17	18	19	20	21	22	23
24	25	26	27	28	29	30

	OCTOBER					
S	M	T	W	T	F	S
1	2	3	4	5	6	7
8	9	10	11	12	13	14
15	16	17	18	19	20	21
22	23	24	25	26	27	28
29	30	31				

	NOVEMBER					
S	M	T	W	T	F	S
			1	2	3	4
5	6	7	8	9	10	11
12	13	14	15	16	17	18
19	20	21	22	23	24	25
26	27	28	29	30		

	DECEMBER					
S	M	T	W	T	F	S
					1	2
3	4	5	6	7	8	9
10	11	12	13	14	15	16
17	18	19	20	21	22	23
24	25	26	27	28	29	30
31						

IMPORTANT DATES

all Jewish holidays begin at sundown the evening before

JANUARY
- 1 New Year's Day
- 17 Martin Luther King Jr. Day

FEBRUARY
- 12 Lincoln's Birthday
- 14 Valentine's Day
- 21 President's Day
- 22 Washington's Birthday

MARCH
- 8 Ash Wednesday
- 17 St. Patrick's Day

APRIL
- 16 Palm Sunday
- 20 Passover
- 21 Good Friday
- 23 Easter Sunday

MAY
- 14 Mother's Day
- 30 Memorial Day

JUNE
- 14 Flag Day
- 18 Father's Day

JULY
- 4 Independence Day

SEPTEMBER
- 4 Labor Day
- 30 Rosh Hannah

OCTOBER
- 9 Yom Kippur
- 9 Columbus Day

NOVEMBER
- 11 Veteran's Day
- 23 Thanksgiving Day

DECEMBER
- 22 Hanukkah
- 25 Christmas Day

89

Jesus Is Coming—A Different Perspective

2001

JANUARY						
S	M	T	W	T	F	S
	1	2	3	4	5	6
7	8	9	10	11	12	13
14	15	16	17	18	19	20
21	22	23	24	25	26	27
28	29	30	31			

FEBRUARY						
S	M	T	W	T	F	S
				1	2	3
4	5	6	7	8	9	10
11	12	13	14	15	16	17
18	19	20	21	22	23	24
25	26	27	28			

MARCH						
S	M	T	W	T	F	S
				1	2	3
4	5	6	7	8	9	10
11	12	13	14	15	16	17
18	19	20	21	22	23	24
25	26	27	28	29	30	31

APRIL						
S	M	T	W	T	F	S
1	2	3	4	5	6	7
8	9	10	11	12	13	14
15	16	17	18	19	20	21
22	23	24	25	26	27	28
29	30					

MAY						
S	M	T	W	T	F	S
		1	2	3	4	5
6	7	8	9	10	11	12
13	14	15	16	17	18	19
20	21	22	23	24	25	26
27	28	29	30	31		

JUNE						
S	M	T	W	T	F	S
					1	2
3	4	5	6	7	8	9
10	11	12	13	14	15	16
17	18	19	20	21	22	23
24	25	26	27	28	29	30

JULY						
S	M	T	W	T	F	S
1	2	3	4	5	6	7
8	9	10	11	12	13	14
15	16	17	18	19	20	21
22	23	24	25	26	27	28
29	30	31				

AUGUST						
S	M	T	W	T	F	S
			1	2	3	4
5	6	7	8	9	10	11
12	13	14	15	16	17	18
19	20	21	22	23	24	25
26	27	28	29	30	31	

SEPTEMBER						
S	M	T	W	T	F	S
						1
2	3	4	5	6	7	8
9	10	11	12	13	14	15
16	17	18	19	20	21	22
23	24	25	26	27	28	29
30						

OCTOBER						
S	M	T	W	T	F	S
	1	2	3	4	5	6
7	8	9	10	11	12	13
14	15	16	17	18	19	20
21	22	23	24	25	26	27
28	29	30	31			

NOVEMBER						
S	M	T	W	T	F	S
				1	2	3
4	5	6	7	8	9	10
11	12	13	14	15	16	17
18	19	20	21	22	23	24
25	26	27	28	29	30	

DECEMBER						
S	M	T	W	T	F	S
						1
2	3	4	5	6	7	8
9	10	11	12	13	14	15
16	17	18	19	20	21	22
23	24	25	26	27	28	29
30	31					

IMPORTANT DATES

All Jewish holidays begin at sundown the evening before

JANUARY
1 New Year's Day
15 Martin Luther King Jr. Day

FEBRUARY
12 Lincoln's Birthday
14 Valentine's Day
19 President's Day
22 Washington's Birthday
28 Ash Wednesday

MARCH
17 St. Patrick's Day

APRIL
8 Palm Sunday
8 Passover
13 Good Friday
15 Easter Sunday

MAY
13 Mother's Day
28 Memorial Day

JUNE
14 Flag Day
17 Father's Day

JULY
4 Independence Day

SEPTEMBER
3 Labor Day
18 Rosh Hashanah
27 Yom Kippur

OCTOBER
12 Columbus Day

NOVEMBER
11 Veteran's Day
22 Thanksgiving Day

DECEMBER
10 Hanukkah
25 Christmas Day

Chapter 4

2002

JANUARY
S	M	T	W	T	F	S
		1	2	3	4	5
6	7	8	9	10	11	12
13	14	15	16	17	18	19
20	21	22	23	24	25	26
27	28	29	30	31		

FEBRUARY
S	M	T	W	T	F	S
					1	2
3	4	5	6	7	8	9
10	11	12	13	14	15	16
17	18	19	20	21	22	23
24	25	26	27	28		

MARCH
S	M	T	W	T	F	S
					1	2
3	4	5	6	7	8	9
10	11	12	13	14	15	16
17	18	19	20	21	22	23
24	25	26	27	28	29	30
31						

APRIL
S	M	T	W	T	F	S
	1	2	3	4	5	6
7	8	9	10	11	12	13
14	15	16	17	18	19	20
21	22	23	24	25	26	27
28	29	30				

MAY
S	M	T	W	T	F	S
			1	2	3	4
5	6	7	8	9	10	11
12	13	14	15	16	17	18
19	20	21	22	23	24	25
26	27	28	29	30	31	

JUNE
S	M	T	W	T	F	S
						1
2	3	4	5	6	7	8
9	10	11	12	13	14	15
16	17	18	19	20	21	22
23	24	25	26	27	28	29
30						

JULY
S	M	T	W	T	F	S
	1	2	3	4	5	6
7	8	9	10	11	12	13
14	15	16	17	18	19	20
21	22	23	24	25	26	27
28	29	30	31			

AUGUST
S	M	T	W	T	F	S
				1	2	3
4	5	6	7	8	9	10
11	12	13	14	15	16	17
18	19	20	21	22	23	24
25	26	27	28	29	30	31

SEPTEMBER
S	M	T	W	T	F	S
1	2	3	4	5	6	7
8	9	10	11	12	13	14
15	16	17	18	19	20	21
22	23	24	25	26	27	28
29	30					

OCTOBER
S	M	T	W	T	F	S
		1	2	3	4	5
6	7	8	9	10	11	12
13	14	15	16	17	18	19
20	21	22	23	24	25	26
27	28	29	30	31		

NOVEMBER
S	M	T	W	T	F	S
					1	2
3	4	5	6	7	8	9
10	11	12	13	14	15	16
17	18	19	20	21	22	23
24	25	26	27	28	29	30

DECEMBER
S	M	T	W	T	F	S
1	2	3	4	5	6	7
8	9	10	11	12	13	14
15	16	17	18	19	20	21
22	23	24	25	26	27	28
29	30	31				

IMPORTANT DATES
All Jewish holidays begin at sundown the evening before

JANUARY
1 New Year's Day
15 Martin Luther King Jr. Day

FEBRUARY
12 Lincoln's Birthday
13 Ash Wednesday
14 Valentine's Day
18 President's Day
22 Washington's Birthday

MARCH
17 St. Patrick's Day
24 Palm Sunday
25 Passover

27 Good Friday
31 Easter Sunday

MAY
12 Mother's Day
27 Memorial Day

JUNE
14 Flag Day
16 Father's Day

JULY
4 Independence Day

SEPTEMBER
2 Labor Day
7 Rosh Hashanah
16 Yom Kippur

OCTOBER
12 Columbus Day

NOVEMBER
11 Veteran's Day
28 Thanksgiving Day
30 Hanukkah

DECEMBER
25 Christmas Day

Jesus Is Coming—A Different Perspective

2003

	JANUARY							FEBRUARY							MARCH					
S	M	T	W	T	F	S	S	M	T	W	T	F	S	S	M	T	W	T	F	S
			1	2	3	4							1							1
5	6	7	8	9	10	11	2	3	4	5	6	7	8	2	3	4	5	6	7	8
12	13	14	15	16	17	18	9	10	11	12	13	14	15	9	10	11	12	13	14	15
19	20	21	22	23	24	25	16	17	18	19	20	21	22	16	17	18	19	20	21	22
26	27	28	29	30	31		23	24	25	26	27	28		23	24	25	26	27	28	29
														30	31					

	APRIL							MAY							JUNE					
S	M	T	W	T	F	S	S	M	T	W	T	F	S	S	M	T	W	T	F	S
		1	2	3	4	5					1	2	3	1	2	3	4	5	6	7
6	7	8	9	10	11	12	4	5	6	7	8	9	10	8	9	10	11	12	13	14
13	14	15	16	17	18	19	11	12	13	14	15	16	17	15	16	17	18	19	20	21
20	21	22	23	24	25	26	18	19	20	21	22	23	24	22	23	24	25	26	27	28
27	28	29	30				25	26	27	28	29	30	31	29	30					

	JULY							AUGUST							SEPTEMBER					
S	M	T	W	T	F	S	S	M	T	W	T	F	S	S	M	T	W	T	F	S
		1	2	3	4	5						1	2		1	2	3	4	5	6
6	7	8	9	10	11	12	3	4	5	6	7	8	9	7	8	9	10	11	12	13
13	14	15	16	17	18	19	10	11	12	13	14	15	16	14	15	16	17	18	19	20
20	21	22	23	24	25	26	17	18	19	20	21	22	23	21	22	23	24	25	26	27
27	28	29	30	31			24	25	26	27	28	29	30	28	29	30				
							31													

	OCTOBER							NOVEMBER							DECEMBER					
S	M	T	W	T	F	S	S	M	T	W	T	F	S	S	M	T	W	T	F	S
			1	2	3	4							1		1	2	3	4	5	6
5	6	7	8	9	10	11	2	3	4	5	6	7	8	7	8	9	10	11	12	13
12	13	14	15	16	17	18	9	10	11	12	13	14	15	14	15	16	17	18	19	20
19	20	21	22	23	24	25	16	17	18	19	20	21	22	21	22	23	24	25	26	27
26	27	28	29	30	31		23	24	25	26	27	28	29	28	29	30	31			
							30													

IMPORTANT DATES

All Jewish holidays begin at sundown the evening before

JANUARY
1 New Year's Day
20 Martin Luther King Jr. Day

FEBRUARY
12 Lincoln's Birthday
14 Valentine's Day
17 President's Day
22 Washington's Birthday

MARCH
5 Ash Wednesday
17 St. Patrick's Day

APRIL
13 Palm Sunday
17 Passover
18 Good Friday
20 Easter Sunday

MAY
11 Mother's Day
26 Memorial Day

JUNE
14 Flag Day
15 Father's Day

JULY
4 Independence Day

SEPTEMBER
1 Labor Day
27 Rosh Hashanah

OCTOBER
6 Yom Kippur
12 Columbus Day

NOVEMBER
11 Veteran's Day
27 Thanksgiving Day

DECEMBER
20 Hanukkah
25 Christmas Day

92

Chapter 4

2004

	JANUARY							FEBRUARY							MARCH					
S	M	T	W	T	F	S	S	M	T	W	T	F	S	S	M	T	W	T	F	S
				1	2	3	1	2	3	4	5	6	7		1	2	3	4	5	6
4	5	6	7	8	9	10	8	9	10	11	12	13	14	7	8	9	10	11	12	13
11	12	13	14	15	16	17	15	16	17	18	19	20	21	14	15	16	17	18	19	20
18	19	20	21	22	23	24	22	23	24	25	26	27	28	21	22	23	24	25	26	27
25	26	27	28	29	30	31	29							28	29	30	31			

	APRIL							MAY							JUNE					
S	M	T	W	T	F	S	S	M	T	W	T	F	S	S	M	T	W	T	F	S
				1	2	3							1			1	2	3	4	5
4	5	6	7	8	9	10	2	3	4	5	6	7	8	6	7	8	9	10	11	12
11	12	13	14	15	16	17	9	10	11	12	13	14	15	13	14	15	16	17	18	19
18	19	20	21	22	23	24	16	17	18	19	20	21	22	20	21	22	23	24	25	26
25	26	27	28	29	30		23	24	25	26	27	28	29	27	28	29	30			
							30	31												

	JULY							AUGUST							SEPTEMBER					
S	M	T	W	T	F	S	S	M	T	W	T	F	S	S	M	T	W	T	F	S
				1	2	3	1	2	3	4	5	6	7				1	2	3	4
4	5	6	7	8	9	10	8	9	10	11	12	13	14	5	6	7	8	9	10	11
11	12	13	14	15	16	17	15	16	17	18	19	20	21	12	13	14	15	16	17	18
18	19	20	21	22	23	24	22	23	24	25	26	27	28	19	20	21	22	23	24	25
25	26	27	28	29	30	31	29	30	31					26	27	28	29	30		

	OCTOBER							NOVEMBER							DECEMBER					
S	M	T	W	T	F	S	S	M	T	W	T	F	S	S	M	T	W	T	F	S
					1	2		1	2	3	4	5	6				01	2	3	4
3	4	5	6	7	8	9	7	8	9	10	11	12	13	5	6	7	8	9	10	11
10	11	12	13	14	15	16	14	15	16	17	18	19	20	12	13	14	15	16	17	18
17	18	19	20	21	22	23	21	22	23	24	25	26	27	19	20	21	22	23	24	25
24	25	26	27	28	29	30	28	29	30					26	27	28	29	30	31	
31																				

IMPORTANT DATES — *All Jewish holidays begin at sundown the evening before*

JANUARY
1 New Year's Day
19 Martin Luther King Jr. Day

FEBRUARY
12 Lincoln's Birthday
14 Valentine's Day
16 President's Day
22 Washington's Birthday
25 Ash Wednesday

MARCH
17 St. Patrick's Day

APRIL
4 Palm Sunday
6 Passover
9 Good Friday
11 Easter Sunday

MAY
9 Mother's Day
31 Memorial Day

JUNE
14 Flag Day
20 Father's Day

JULY
4 Independence Day

SEPTEMBER
6 Labor Day
15 Rosh Hashanah
25 Yom Kippur

OCTOBER
12 Columbus Day

NOVEMBER
11 Veteran's Day
25 Thanksgiving Day

DECEMBER
8 Hanukkah
25 Christmas Day

93

Jesus Is Coming—A Different Perspective

The Calculations

2004
April	6 days
March	31 days
February	29 days
January	31 days

2004 Total — 97 days

2003 — + 365 days

2002 — + 365 days

2001 — + 365 days

2000
December	31 days
November	30 days
October	31 days
September	1 days

2000 Total — + 93 days

Total Calendar Calculation = 1285 days

Anticipated Time Line − 1260 days

25 days off

CHAPTER 5

NOTES ON DANIEL 11

In this fifth chapter, I have used the material compiled in this book to help interpret Daniel, Chapter 11. In the light of the end-time circumstances, which the angel told Daniel would befall his people at the end of the age, we have been given insight into that which will befall us Christians right up to the time the Lord calls us at the rapture. Many may criticize this effort, but I do so to demonstrate that the Church should be thinking along this line of reasoning.

Preface to Daniel 11

In Chapter 10 of Daniel, an angel explains to Daniel, *Now I am come to make thee understand what shall befall thy people in the latter days: for yet the vision is for many days* (Daniel 10:14) and *But I will shew thee that which is noted in the scripture of truth:*

and there is none that holdeth with me in these things, but Michael your prince (Daniel 10:21). It is important to understand that some prophecies serve a dual function in that some are for the present or near future and some are for a time which is far in the future. We Christians and Jews can see the historical evidence of a great God who knows the beginning of things on to the end of everything. We can glorify the God of creation by knowing and giving testimony of the near prophecies of scriptures that have already been accomplished. Today we are in a position where we will see many future prophecies fulfilled. The end of the age is now upon us. During Daniel's time, it was made clear that world powers would be given free reign to develop, with Satan in control, throughout the world's systems. This period is called "time of the Gentiles." During this time, the Jews were a witness that there is a God that requires all mankind to know Him. Approximately two thousand years ago, God created a new creation of mankind; they were called saints, holy people, Christians. These Christians joined the Jews in declaring that this God, who is both a loving and a just God, requires that all know Him and receive justice through Him.

Another important fact that should be understood before we continue with Daniel 11 is the location of nations in relation to how God sees them. When God speaks of things upon the earth, He always measures from Israel, because Israel is His earthly center. The powers which deal with Israel are, in God's view, those that are important. This is the reason the newer kingdoms of today from Alexander's destroyed empire are not mentioned. Only those kingdoms of the north and south are dealt with. Why are they so described?

Chapter 5

Palestine is the land from which God judges. The king of the north means north of the land that His eyes rest upon, and the southern power means south of that same land. These are the countries commonly called Syria and Egypt in Daniel and Isaiah's day and Russia and the United Nations today. Why is it that the king of the south is the one who heads the United Nations? I believe it is because most of the member nations, at least ninety percent, lie south of Israel.

I think that one more observation should be stated before looking at scripture. From Daniel 11:5 onward, the scripture contains prophecies which have been fulfilled or are soon to be fulfilled. The interpretation of these verses requires that all scripture follow the outline of these verses. My attempt to be accurate, but still include other scriptures, is fallible. I am human and not God, and as a result, the interpretation given is definitely subject to error. It is my endeavor to give what I think is a plausible explanation of each verse, though it is possible that someone else will provide better scriptural reasoning than I have.

The Text of Daniel 11

Using the King James Version of the Bible, I have asked God to bless this attempt in seeking truth about the prophecies of Daniel 11. The entirety of the text, with my comments and interpretations, follows:

Verses 1-4: *Also I, in the first year of Darius the Mede, even I, [the angel] stood to confirm and to strengthen him [Daniel]. And now will I shew thee the truth. Behold, there shall stand up yet three kings in Persia; and the fourth shall be far richer than they all: and by his strength through his riches he shall stir up all against the realm of Grecia. And a mighty king shall stand up, that shall rule with great dominion, and do according to his will. And when he shall stand up, his kingdom shall be broken, and shall be divided toward the four winds of heaven; and not to his posterity, nor according to his dominion which he ruled: for his kingdom shall be plucked up, even for others beside those.*

Comment: Starting in verse one, the angel gives the time he is giving this revelation to Daniel. Then the angel gives a rapid survey of world events that occurs before he tells Daniel what would befall Israel in the latter days. The angel gives a quick glance to the near future that will lead to details of end-time events starting with verse five. The three kings mentioned in verse two are revealed in Ezra Chapter four. Alexander the Great is the fourth king mentioned.

Most commentators give an historical interpretation of verses 5 through 36, ascribing these verses to Antiochus Epiphanes. However, the angel said he would give Daniel the understanding from that which is contained in the scripture of truth regarding "the latter days." Thus, beginning with verse 5, we begin to understand how the Jew and the Christian are affected today.

Verse 5: *And the king of the south shall be strong, and one of his princes; and he shall be strong above him, and have dominion; his dominion shall be a great dominion.*

Chapter 5

Comment: The king of the south shall be strong. This king is the person who heads the United Nations. This organization began in June 1945. The verse states this king shall be strong in the future tense. The prince that is stronger above him is, of course, the United States.

Verse 6: *And in the end of years they shall join themselves together; for the king's daughter of the south shall come to the king of the north to make an agreement: but she shall not retain the power of the arm; neither shall he stand, nor his arm: but she shall be given up, and they that brought her, and he that begat her, and he that strengthened her in these times.*

Comment: An overall picture of this king's daughter of the south, the world's financial system, is given in Revelation 17 and 18. During the generation which will see the end of the age, this financial system is centered in the United States. Those who control this financial system negotiated an agreement with the king of the north, which resulted in the break up of the Soviet Union. This agreement also brought an end to the "cold war" or "iron curtain" conditions. These conditions, which caused great suffering for all its citizens and Russian-occupied countries, also prevented Russia from enjoying economic growth after World War II. All who have anything to do with this worldly system will eventually be judged and given up. Its final destruction will be on the Day of Wrath at the seventh trumpet. It will meet its end in one hour.

Verse 7: *But out of a branch of her roots shall one stand up in his estate, which shall come with an army, and shall enter into the fortress of the king of the north, and shall deal against them, and shall prevail.*

Comment: The last branch of the financial system will emerge and conquer the stronghold of Russia. Russia has given up the occupied countries of Europe but has maintained a strong influence over some Middle Eastern countries, including Iran. From the time of the Cold War up to this very day, Russia has influenced Iran's government with military advice and financial support. Thus, I consider Iran to be a fortress of Russia. It is my belief that the incident that initiates military action will be the second trumpet of Revelation 8:8-9. A nuclear missile will explode in the Persian Gulf. The United States' naval fleet, along with other allied ships, is centered in this area. To avoid nuclear retaliation, the offending country will be blackmailed into accomplishing the actions of the following verse.

Verse 8: And shall also carry captive into Egypt their gods, with their princes, and with their precious vessels of silver and of gold; and he shall continue more years than the king of the north.

Comment: The gods referred to here are the Ayatollahs who rule over the civil authorities of Iran. Iran has a national treasure second to no other nation on earth. The Ayatollahs, the civil leaders, and its national treasure will be taken into Egypt. For a number of years, the Iranians, with other militant Moslem (Muslim) leaders have attempted to bring down the government of Egypt because of their liberal interpretation of the Moslem faith. Because

Chapter 5

of the aggressive action mentioned in the above comment, I believe the United States will be the nation accomplishing this nearly bloodless siege. It will command the surrender of Iran's leaders and the seizure of its gods and treasures at a certain place, probably its capitol. If this is not done, the whole city will be destroyed with one swift missile deployment. After the 70th week is over and the millennial reign begins, the United States will still be in existence, but Russia will not.

Verse 9: *So the king of the south shall come into his kingdom, and shall return into his own land.*

Comment: The leader of the United Nations will travel to Washington and discuss the events with the President and other politicians. After the meeting, he will leave the United States and return to one of the U.N. buildings or to his homeland, which would be Africa if this event happened today.

Verse 10: *But his sons shall be stirred up, and shall assemble a multitude of great forces: and one shall certainly come, and overflow, and pass through: then shall he return, and be stirred up, even to his fortress.*

Comment: It appears that the presence of the United States in the Middle East is gone. After the nuclear attack on its ships and the subsequent conquering of Iran, the United States leaves the area to let whatever happens to happen. Many of the United Nation's members (sons) will be stirred up and will assemble a multitude of great forces comprised of the armies of each nation. In today's structure, this great force could be the European

Union, along with Russia. The "one" referred to in the verse is Russia. Acting alone, without the assembled great forces, it will come and perform the action of the "one" in verse 15.

Verse 11: *And the king of the south shall be moved with choler (anger), and shall come forth and fight with him, even with the king of the north: and he shall set forth a great multitude; but the multitude shall be given into his hand.*

Comment: The United Nations, acting as a whole unit and probably backed by the United States, will go into the Middle East to confront the multitudes. When this happens, all will back off except Russia. Russia continues to acquire support, perhaps from some of the Middle East countries such as Edom, Moab, and the chief of the children of Ammon. This multitude will be given temporarily into the U.N.'s hands after Russia's action in verse 15. When the king of the south goes forth to fight, I speculate that it will be at this time that a treaty will be made with Israel. The U.N. will occupy Jerusalem to ensure peace. This treaty will later be confirmed by the Antichrist.

Verse 12: *And when he hath taken away the multitude, his heart shall be lifted up; and he shall cast down many ten thousands: but he shall not be strengthened by it.*

Comment: Initially, the U.N. will be successful and will be allowed to remain in the Middle East. This success will be short-lived; however, the end of the age will have arrived.

Chapter 5

Verse 13: *For the king of the north shall return, and shall set forth a multitude greater than the former, and shall certainly come after certain years with a great army and with much riches.*

Comment: We should stop and reflect on what has happened to this point. The second trumpet in verse seven initiates everything that follows. At this point, the 70th week has started and will reach its halfway point soon. On the 1260th day, the end of the age occurs, and God's wrath is dispensed over the whole earth. All that occurs from verse seven to the end of this chapter will occur in 3-1/2 years. On the 2300th day of the 70th week, the Gog-Magog battle, referred to in this verse, will occur.

Verse 14: *And in those times there shall many stand up against the king of the south: also the robbers of thy people shall exalt themselves to establish the vision: but they shall fall.*

Comment: It has been seen in history over and over again. Whenever there is a successful campaign, those who were opposed or uninvolved with the campaign shout, "Unfair; down with the victors." This occurred when the U. S. invaded Iraq, and it will happen with the U.N.'s success. Many members of the U.N. and others on the outside will demand withdrawal and concession of the war area. Among those objecting will be the Palestinian Moslems (referred to in the verse as "the robbers of thy people"). This group will attempt to defeat the occupying forces, but they will fail. It is my belief that they will sink into insignificance after this failed attempt to gain power.

Verse 15: *So the king of the north shall come, and cast up a mount, and take the most fenced cities: and the arms of the south shall not withstand, neither his chosen people, neither shall there be any strength to withstand.*

Comment: This action by the king of the north (Russia) begins as a blitz action. The angel is telling Daniel what will befall his people at the end of the age, but this action and subsequent events affect the surrounding Middle Eastern countries as well as Israel. This quick action will occur at a time when the Israelites feel secure, and it will take them and everyone by surprise. Perhaps this is the incident in which Zechariah 14:2 is accomplished, at least in part. This swift action seems to bog down before the king of the north reaches Egypt. "His chosen people" in the verse is probably referring to Iran, who will have lost its leadership and will not be effective in supporting the king of the north. This will give enough time, as long as a year or two, for the False Prophet and the Antichrist to rise to power.

The Rise of the False Prophet

Verse 16: *But he that cometh against him shall do according to his own will, and none shall stand before him: and he shall stand in the glorious land, which by his hand shall be consumed.*

Comment: It is interesting that the False Prophet allows the king of the north to do as he wishes. Evidently, the False Prophet does not engage in battle with the king of the north. He consults with

Chapter 5

and advises all the groups in the area to regroup, consolidate, and unite. He appears to be attempting to make a bad situation better than it was before the blitz action occurred. The U.N. forces were present when the king of the north blitzed the area, but its peace efforts failed to protect the people. The unified group allows the False Prophet to enter Israel and become the authority for this area. He is placed in control of the U.N. forces as well as of the fortified and unified group. The False Prophet will not be a part of the peoples of this area. He will be an outsider who is endowed with great diplomatic skill.

Verse 17: He shall also set his face to enter with the strength of his whole kingdom, and upright ones with him; thus shall he do: and he shall give him the daughter of women, corrupting her: but she shall not stand on his side, neither be for him.

Comment: When the False Prophet first enters the Middle East after the Russian blitz, he will probably be sent as a negotiator to smooth the emotional turmoil. During the process of securing the nations and providing a defense against Russia reentering their countries, he is able to get total control of Israel. By the time he enters Israel, his authority comes not only from the newly united confederacy but also from his original authority. He has the full backing from the government he represents and probably from the United Nations. He will have enough authority to present a financial structure (daughter of woman) to the Antichrist. This is the financial system mentioned in verse 6 as the king's daughter of the south. I believe that this financial system is centered in the United States. The False Prophet probably comes from the United States and works for the United Nations, which would explain his ability to convey the financial control of the world to the Antichrist. The "upright ones" will be influential persons from the United States Congress and key United Nations personnel whose goal will be to secure world peace.

Verse 18: *After this shall he turn his face unto the isles, and shall take many: but a prince for his own behalf shall cause the reproach offered by him to cease; without his own reproach he shall cause it to turn upon him.*

Comment: After becoming a hero to Israel and the other confederate countries, he will make a mistake by attacking the isles, perhaps Cyprus or Greece. His popularity will wane, and his power will reduce. The individual who takes his place and attempts to continue the False Prophet's plans will also lose popularity.

Verse 19: *Then he shall turn his face toward the fort of his own land: but he shall stumble and fall, and not be found.*

Comment: This fallen hero will decide to return to the security of his homeland; however, he will not arrive. I envision a plane crash from which his body will not be found. He disappears, and he will be missing for some time.

Chapter 5

The Rise of the Antichrist

Verse 20: Then shall stand up in his estate a raiser of taxes in the glory of the kingdom: but within few days he shall be destroyed, neither in anger, nor in battle.

Comment: An individual who is known for his ability to raise funds to help finance the activities of the confederate forces will assume the position of leadership. In a very short time, he also will lose his powerful position. This is probably due to the shifting of power within the confederacy. I believe this person is from Jerusalem since it could be referred to as "the glory of the kingdom."

Verse 21: And in his estate shall stand up a vile person, to whom they shall not give the honor of the kingdom: but he shall come in peaceably, and obtain the kingdom by flatteries.

Comment: The individual called the "raiser of taxes" in verse 20 will be replaced by a person who is not favored. He is an evil person, but he will appear to be peaceful and benign. At first, his speeches will be filled with complimentary words and uplifting phrases. He will give himself the title of king of Israel. This is the Antichrist.

Verse 22: And with the arms of a flood shall they be overflown from before him, and shall be broken; yea, also the prince of the covenant.

Comment: As the Antichrist gains control over the nation of Israel and the surrounding areas of the Middle East, these areas will revert to the same conditions that existed when Jesus walked the area with His disciples. They will go back to a time when they were not in control and authority was exerted upon them by force. I often wonder if the False Prophet and the Antichrist will be signers of the pact that brings the False Prophet into power.

Verse 23: *And after the league made with him he shall work deceitfully: for he shall come up, and shall become strong with a small people.*

Comment: As the Antichrist proceeds with his control over the people, an elite group will gain power. This may be some kind of financial cartel. The composition of the group is unclear, but it is known that the Antichrist is deceitful in his quest for power and position.

Verse 24: *He shall enter peaceably even upon the fattest places of the province; and he shall do that which his fathers have not done, nor his father's fathers; he shall scatter among them the prey, and spoil, and riches; yea, and he shall forecast his devices against the strongholds, even for a time.*

Comment: The Antichrist will cajole his way into areas that have had relatively little trouble. He will do things that his father and his father's father did not do. He will gain control of the confederate defense pact. He will scatter spoils of war and wealth throughout the area but will also install devices that will destroy these same people. I believe that the Antichrist is an Israelite because the scripture speaks of the inability of his father and grandfather to enter these areas in peace.

Chapter 5

Verse 25: *And he shall stir up his power and his courage against the king of the south with a great army; and the king of the south shall be stirred up to battle with a very great and mighty army; but he shall not stand: for they shall forecast devices against him.*

Comment: The Antichrist will boldly challenge the power of the king of the south (the United Nations). The king of the south will have a mighty army deployed to the area, but the fighting will be delayed. I suspect this delay is due to political maneuvering and threats of atomic destruction.

Verse 26: *Yea, they that feed of the portion of his meat shall destroy him, and his army shall overflow: and many shall fall down slain.*

Comment: The Antichrist and his confederation will control the oil in desert and arid lands. Since the people cannot eat oil, they will import most of their food. Food will come from the nations that belong to the United Nations. There will be great turmoil when the nations are oil rich and food poor. Many will die in this area when this struggle occurs. God's wrath will come upon both groups of opposing forces, and they will die. The power of these two forces will be finished.

Verse 27: *And both these kings' hearts shall be to do mischief, and they shall speak lies at one table; but it shall not prosper: for yet the end shall be at the time appointed.*

Comment: Both the king of the south and the Antichrist will create turmoil and confusion. They will speak lies at one table, perhaps at a meeting to form a pack or treaty, but neither will be trusted. Despite their plots and schemes, they will not avoid the time appointed for their destruction, which has been set as the first day of the seventh month on the Jewish calendar.

Verse 28: *Then shall he return into his land with great riches; and his heart shall be against the holy covenant; and he shall do exploits, and return to his own land.*

Comment: The Antichrist will return to his stronghold of power. Perhaps this is the time that verse 24 is implemented. He becomes set in his resolve to defy the holy covenant that God has made with the people of Israel. He manipulates to stop the continuation of the desired peace.

Verse 29: *At the time appointed he shall return, and come toward the south; but it shall not be as the former, or as the latter.*

Comment: By this time, the fourth trumpet will have occurred, and Satan has been cast down to the earth. I believe the Russians have been lurking around Egypt in hopes of being able to continue their stalled blitz. The Antichrist will make warlike gestures to the areas south of Jerusalem. Regardless of the Antichrist's plans, God's timetable is progressing forward.

Verse 30: *For the ships of Chittim shall come against him: therefore he shall be grieved, and return, and have indignation against the holy covenant: so shall he do; he shall even return, and have intelligence with them that forsake the holy covenant.*

Chapter 5

Comment: I am told that Russia has a large naval station with nuclear submarines on Cyprus, an island close to Greece. Cyprus is given two names in the Bible: Chittim and Kittim. When the Antichrist begins to move south, he will be threatened with this power and confronted by Russian armaments on the sea and in the south. He returns to Jerusalem with a more bitter resolve to thwart the holy covenant. He schemes and draws Jews from the areas to create a group of apostate Jews.

Judgment on the Antichrist

Zechariah 11:17 states, *Woe to the idol shepherd that leaveth the flock! The sword shall be upon his arm, and upon his right eye: his arm shall be clean dried up, and his right eye shall be utterly darkened.* This passage is referring to the Antichrist. I believe that an assassination attempt or an actual battle will occur in which the Antichrist will be gravely injured. To the amazement of the world, the False Prophet will re-appear and support the Antichrist. I believe that Satan has possessed the False Prophet and is acting through him to complete the destruction of the Jews (Revelation 12:13-17). The activities of the False Prophet are described in Revelation 13:11-18.

Verse 31: *And arms shall stand on his part, and they shall pollute the sanctuary of strength and shall take away the daily sacrifice, and they shall place the abomination that maketh desolate.*

Comment: In previous verses, the pronoun "he" is used; here in this verse, the pronoun is "they." The world becomes sympathetic to the Antichrist when he receives such a terrible injury. There is a further surprise when the False Prophet appears. Satan allows the False Prophet to perform miracles while in the presence of the Antichrist. With such potent power, they proceed to desecrate the sanctuary (the holy place), take away the daily sacrifices (prayer and thanksgiving to God), and set up an abomination that destroys the very purpose of the temple. An image of the Antichrist will be placed in the sanctuary. I do not believe that this sanctuary is a newly built temple. According to Acts 15:14-17, the new temple will be built after the resurrection of the Church.

The Abomination That Maketh Desolate

It is important to note that the False Prophet, indwelled by Satan, has the power to make this image of the Antichrist speak and declare a death sentence on those who do not worship this image. We are told that when the image is set up and the Antichrist is revealed, there will be a time of great tribulation. Paul taught us that the Church would not be raptured until after the Antichrist is revealed. The act of setting up the idol will positively identify the Antichrist. Daniel teaches us that when the idol is set up, there will be 1290 days to the end of the 70th week, which means we Christians will be here when the abomination that maketh desolate is set up. We are taught in Revelation 7:14 that the raptured

Chapter 5

church is taken out of the Great Tribulation period and enters in before the throne of God. The act of setting up the image occurs 30 days before the middle of the 70th week. This will be the end of the age. Our rapture will be in the middle of the 70th week. God's Day of Wrath will be in the middle of the 70th week and will bring an end to the time of the Gentiles.

God speaks to the "they" in Isaiah 28 and 29, *Wherefore hear the word of the Lord, ye scornful men that rule this people which are in Jerusalem. Because ye have said, we have made a covenant with death, and with hell are we at agreement; when the overflowing scourge shall pass through, it shall not come upon us: for we have made lies our refuge, and under falsehood have we hid ourselves. And your covenant with death shall be disannulled, and your agreement with hell shall not stand; when the overflowing scourge shall pass through, then ye shall be trodden down by it* (Isaiah 28:14-15, 18). The overflowing scourge will be the armies of the kings of the East.

Verse 32: *And such as do wickedly against the covenant shall he corrupt by flatteries: but the people that do know their God shall be strong, and do exploits.*

Comment: Those who work against the holy covenant will be congratulated for their change of thought. Many will rationalize their decision to change their previous stand. God said that would happen. The propaganda from the evil trio (the False Prophet, the Antichrist, and Satan) is forcefully foisted upon the world.

The People Who Know Their God: The Two Witnesses

Verse 33-35: *And they that understand among the people shall instruct many: yet they shall fall by the sword, and by flame, by captivity, and by spoil many days. Now when they shall fall, they shall be holpen with a little help: but many shall cleave to them with flatteries. And some of them of understanding shall fall, to try them, and to purge, and to make them white, even to the time of the end: because it is yet for a time appointed.*

Comment: Those Christians and Jews who have understanding about this time will instruct the less informed. Some will die. There is a cleansing for many, and many others will be martyrs. If there is any confusion, reread the section in Chapter 3 entitled "The Two Witnesses."

The King

Verses 36-39: *And the king shall do according to his will; and he shall exalt himself, and magnify himself above every god, and shall speak marvelous things against the God of gods, and shall prosper till the indignation be accomplished: for that that is determined shall be done. Neither shall he regard the God of his fathers, nor the desire of women, nor regard any god: for he shall magnify himself above all. But in his estate shall he honour the God of forces: and a god*

Chapter 5

whom his father knew not shall he honour with gold, and silver, and with precious stones, and pleasant things. Thus shall he do in the most strongholds with a strange god, whom he shall acknowledge and increase with glory: and he shall cause them to rule over many, and shall divide the land for gain.

Comment: The Antichrist will take the title of king in an attempt to take the place of the true King, our Savior.

The book *Lectures on the Book of Daniel*, written before World War I by William Kelly, is a treasure unknown to many people today. At the time of his writing, Mr. Kelly had no knowledge of when Israel would become a nation again. Following is a quote from pages 220-227 of the third edition, published by Loizeaux Brother, Bible Truth Depot, 19 West 21st Street, New York.

"For now, in verse 36, we have another person abruptly introduced into the scene. We are not told who he was, or whence he came; but the character that is given of him, the scene that he occupies, the history that the Spirit of God enters into in connection with him—all declare, too plainly, that it is the terrible king who set himself up in the land of Israel in personal antagonism to the Messiah of Israel, the returning Lord. He it was of whom our Lord spoke when He said that if they refused Him who had come in His Father's name, they would receive another coming in his own name. Nor is this the only passage of Scripture where this same false Christ, or rather Antichrist (for there is a

115

difference between the terms) is described as "the king." Not only are there different references to him under other epithets, but in the greatest and most comprehensive prophecy of Scripture, Isaiah, like Daniel, introduces "the king" as if he must be known at once.

"In Chapter 30, we have an enemy of Israel called the Assyrian. Doubtless, looking at past history, Sennacherib was their great head in that day. But he only furnished the opportunity to the Spirit of God to bring out the future and final adversary of Israel. His fall is here brought before us. *For through the voice of Jehovah shall the Assyrian be beaten down who smote with a rod. And in every place where the grounded staff shall pass, which Jehovah shall lay upon him, it shall be with tabrets and harps: and in battles of shaking will He fight with it.* After the end of that victory there will be exceeding joy for Israel; instead of the train of sorrow which most victories bring, there follows unfeigned gladness before Jehovah. *It shall be with tabrets and harps.* For the enemy there will be proportionate misery. Something still more awful and unending than temporal destruction falls upon the proud foe. *For Tophet is ordained of old, yea, for the king it is prepared: He hath made it deep and large; the pile thereof is fire and much wood; the breach of Jehovah, like a stream of brimstone, doth kindle it.* In our version, there is a singular obscurity, remarked by another, in this verse. At first sight it might appear that the Assyrian and "the king" was the same person. The true rendering is, *For the king also it is prepared;* that is, Tophet is

Chapter 5

prepared for the Assyrian, but, besides, for THE KING also; just as in our passage in Daniel we have the Assyrian, or king of the north, on the one hand, and "the king" on the other. The same frightful end awaits then both.

"But I refer to this now only for the purpose of showing that the expression "the king" is not unprecedented in Scripture and that it applies to a notorious personage the Jews were taught in prophecy to expect. God, in judicial retribution for their rejection of the true Christ, would give them up to receive the Antichrist. This is "the king." He would arrogate to himself the royal rights of the true King, the Anointed of God. Tophet was prepared for the king of the north, and also for "the king."

"But this is not all. In Isaiah 57, we have him introduced quite as unexpectedly. In Chapter 56 are shown the moral qualities that God will produce in His people. In Chapter 57, we hear of the fearfully iniquitous state then also found in Israel. And in that day, God will no longer endure anything but reality. Forms of piety, covering uncleanness and ungodliness, will give way to apostasy. Then "the king" is suddenly introduced to us (verse 9). *Thou wentest to the king with ointment, and didst increase thy perfumes, and didst send thy messengers far off, and didst debase thyself unto hell.* To have to do with him was to debase oneself unto hell. No wonder that for "the king also" Tophet was prepared. This shows that, from the first, the Spirit of God led the mind of

Israel to expect a lawless one to reign over the land in the last days, who is called "the king."

"Thus at once is furnished a most important clue to Daniel 11. We are come to the time of the end. The blank is closed—the long dark night of Israel's dispersion is well nigh over. The Jews are in the land. In what condition? Are they under Christ? Alas! There is another and a terrible scene that must first be enacted there. "The king" that we have read of is there, and the course he pursues is just what we might expect from the landmarks of the Holy Ghost. *The king shall do according to his will.* Ah! Are any of us sufficiently aware what a fearful thing it is to be the doers of our will? Here is the end of self-will. It was the first great characteristic of sin from the beginning. It is what Adam did, and his fall and the ruin of the world were the immediate result. Here is one who at that day may seem to be the loftiest and most influential of men. But he does *according to his will.* And nothing worse. Are we to read such a history as this without moral profit to our own souls? To forget what an evil thing it is ever to be the doers of our own will? Let none suppose that because they may be in a position to rule, they are therefore outside the danger. Alas! It is not so: no one thing so unfits a person for righteous rule as the inability to obey. It is good first to know what it is to be subject. Oh, may it strike deep into all our hearts that "the king," the Antichrist, is first stamped as one doing his own will! May it test us how far we are seeking ours!—how far, under any circumstances, we are doing or allowing anything that we would not wish every soul in this

Chapter 5

world to see—perhaps even those that are nearest to us.

"Alas! One knows from experience and observation the difficulty and danger in these things from one's own heart. Yet there is no one thing more contrary to that Christ whom we have learnt. We are sanctified *unto the obedience and sprinkling of the blood of Jesus Christ*. It is not only to the blessing in the sprinkling of the blood, but to the obedience of Jesus Christ—to the same spirit and principle of obedience; for this is the meaning of the expression. We are not like the Jews who were put under law, and whose obedience had the character of obligation to do such and such things under penalty of death. We are already alive unto God, conscious of the blessedness in which we stand, and awakened to see the beauty of the will of God; for His will it is which has saved and sanctified us. This is our calling, and our practical work here below. Christians have no other business, properly speaking, than to do the will of another. We have to do God's will according to the character of the obedience of Christ—as sons delighting in the will of the Father. It does not matter what we may have to do. It may be one's natural daily occupation. But do not make two individuals of yourselves—with one principle in your business or family, and another for the Church and worship of God. Never allow such a thought. We have Christ for everything and every day.

"Christ is not a blessing for us merely when we meet together or are called to die; but if we have Christ, we have Him forever, and from the first moment, we are emancipated from doing our own will. This we learn is death; but it is gone now in

Christ's death. We are delivered, for we are alive in Him risen. But what are we delivered for? To do the will of God. We are sanctified unto the obedience of Jesus Christ.

"As for 'the king,' you have in him the awful principle of sin which has always been at work, but which here exceeds all bounds. The moment will have come when God will remove the providential checks which, up to that time, He will have put upon men, when Satan will be allowed to bring about all his plans; and that, too, in the very land whereon the eyes of God rest continually.

"The king shall do according to his own will, and he shall exalt himself and magnify himself—not only above every man, but 'above every god.' And it is not only that he takes his place above these so-called gods, but 'he shall speak marvelous things against the God of gods.' And, strange to say, (if one did not know the perfect wisdom of God, and could not wait for His counsels to be matured,) in spite of his fearful profanity, 'he shall prosper till the indignation be accomplished; for that is determined shall be done.' The clause contains a word that gives us the key to the passage. For some have found immense difficulties in this portion of the word of God. Many have transported into this verse the pope of Rome; others, Mohammed, or Bonaparte. However, here we find that 'the king' is to prosper until the indignation is accomplished. What, or about whom? Has God now indignation against His Church? Never. This is the time, too, of God's patience with man, not of His indignation.

Chapter 5

"With whom, then, is it connected? The Word of God is perfectly plain. It is when dealing with Israel that God speaks of 'indignation': I have already shown this fully from Isaiah 5-10, 14, and other passages, as it is entirely confirmed by the whole nature of the revelation here. For we read of one that would be the king of Israel—not in Constantinople or Rome, but in Palestine. And the time is a future outburst of indignation against Israel in the Promised Land. He (the false king) shall prosper until the indignation be accomplished. Neither shall he regard the God of his fathers, nor the desire of women. The expression 'the desire of women' clearly, to my mind, refers to Christ—the One to whom all Jews were looking forward, and whose birth must have been, above all things, desired by Jewish women. It is plain from the connection that such is the true meaning, for it occurs between 'the God of his fathers' (Jehovah) and 'any god.' Nothing is less likely than, if it had merely referred to natural relationships, that it would have been thus placed. It was, probably, from the wish to apply this to the pope that such as interpretation has found currency. But let us only understand that the prophecy concerns Israel and their land, and all is plain. *He shall not regard the God of his fathers, nor the desire of women.* Christ is distinguished from 'the God of his fathers,' perhaps, because the Son was to become incarnate. But Christ is regarded no more than the God of his fathers—an expression, by the way, which implies that he himself is a Jew. It is *'the God of his fathers.' For he shall magnify himself above all.* But in his *estate shall he honor the god of forces.* It is not that he goes forward as Antiochus did, trying to force Zeus Olympus upon the Jews; but he adopts a new superstition. This also disproves the reference to the Syrian king, who was a Gentile. Here it is a Jew who will take the place of the Christ, and who, of course, regards neither the true Christ nor Jehovah. It is a self-exalting personage who opposes the true God; who equally sets aside the superstitions of men and the faith of God's people. Self-exaltation is his marked feature.

"But this is not all. The Antichrist will be infidel, but not merely infidel. He will have rejected the God of Israel, and the Messiah. Nor will he honor any of the gods of the Gentiles. But even this man, although he sets himself up as God upon the earth, will, for all that, have some one to whom he bows, and causes others to bow along with himself. The human heart, even in Antichrist, cannot do without an object of worship. So in verse 38, there is this apparent inconsistency that comes out in the Antichrist. *But in his estate shall he honor the god of forces.* He makes a god, besides the setting himself up to be God. *A god whom his fathers knew not shall he honor with gold and silver, and with precious stones, and pleasant things.* It is entirely an invention of his own. More than that: he will divide the land among his adherents. *He shall cause them to rule over many, and shall divide the land for gain.* Such, then, is God's account of the king that will be found in Palestine in the last days. And it is plain that this last verse is a most conclusive proof that he is in Palestine reigning. It is "the land." The Sprit of God never so speaks of any other country. It was that land which was nearest to God—a sort of center for all others."

Having presented William Kelly's commentary on verses 36-39, I want to add some of my thoughts to these verses. I believe that Satan is in complete control of the Antichrist and the False Prophet. He was cast down at the fourth trumpet and is here when the seventh trumpet is about to be sounded. Just as he entered into Judas Iscariot (John 13:27), he will enter into the False Prophet. His goal is to eradicate Israel.

Verse 40: *And at the time of the end shall the king of the south push at him: and the king of the north shall come against him like a whirlwind, with chariots, and with horseman, and with many ships; and he shall enter into the countries, and shall overflow and pass over.*

Comment: This is the "Day of the Lord." This is the Resurrection-Wrath day. This is when the time of the Gentiles comes to an end. This is when the king of the south (the United Nations) comes against the Antichrist in Israel (Psalm 2). This is also the day that Russia comes against the Antichrist by land and sea. They will sweep back the way they came earlier. In doing so, Russia will face and destroy the armies of the kings of the east at Armageddon.

Verses 41-44: *He shall enter also into the glorious land, and many countries shall be overthrown: but these shall escape out of his hand, even Edom, and Moab, and the chief of the children of Ammon. He shall stretch forth his hand also upon the countries: and the land of Egypt shall not escape. But he shall have power over the treasures of gold and of silver, and over all the precious things of Egypt: and the Libyans and the Ethiopians shall be at his steps. But tidings out of the east and out of the north shall trouble him: therefore he shall go forth with great fury to destroy, and utterly to make away many.*

> *Comment*: This is a reinstatement of what has already occurred to bring the king of the north against Israel on the Day of Wrath (verse 40).

Verse 45: *And he shall plant the tabernacles of his palace between the seas in the glorious holy mountain; yet he shall come to his end, and none shall help him.*

> *Comment:* In verse 40 it states that Russia shall overflow and pass over on the Day of Wrath. This verse jumps forward approximately three years, when on the 2300th day of the 70th week, at the battle of Gog-Magog, king of the north meets his doom. Tophet (the Lake of Fire) is waiting for him as Mr. Kelly described in his writings. God is so gracious to give us these details of the last 3-1/2 years that end "the time of the Gentiles." The Gog-Magog action upon Israel demonstrates that the time of the Gentiles is finished. At this time, Satan is not cast into Tophet but into the bottomless pit. He will be there until a future time when he is released for a season. Tophet still waits for him. The verses in Revelation 12:15-17 cover the period in Daniel 11:40-45. Revelation 12:15 states, *And the serpent cast out of his mouth water as a flood after the woman (Israel), that he might cause her to be carried away of the flood.* The flood is the armies of the world (the kings of the east, south, and north)

Chapter 5

coming against Israel. Revelation 12:16 states, *And the earth helped the woman, and the earth opened her mouth, and swallowed up the flood which the dragon cast out of his mouth."* God's wrath caused this to happen. *"And the dragon was wroth with the woman, and went to make war with the remnant of her seed, which keep the commandments of God, and have the testimony of Jesus Christ* (Revelation 12:17). This last action will bring about the Gog-Magog type battle described in Ezekiel 38 and 39.

Author's Testimony

My life's story, which led me to salvation and the knowledge of Christ, is one of persistence combined with the influences of many Christians whose names I do not know.

I did not grow up in a Christian home. For some reason, my parents had decided that they would let their children grow up and determine what religious practices they would observe. Both of my grandmothers were Christians. My Grandmother Steele took me to her Methodist Church to attend preschool classes where I probably heard the Name of Jesus for the first time. This experience was not long lasting, but I remember it with pleasure.

We moved to the rural area of Alton, Illinois when I was eight years old. One day I decided to visit a nearby Baptist church where I attended a Sunday school class taught by a man named Bob. He loved the Lord and I sensed his strong relationship with Jesus. I wanted that type of relationship. My desire to know Jesus was fervent and I longed for a father-son relationship with God.

In my early teens, a friend named Tom asked me to go to church with him. It was then that I truly began to grow in the knowledge of Jesus and saw Him not only as a father figure but as my Savior and Lord. I knew that I had to declare this to others. I followed our Lord's instruction and was publicly baptized. I began to declare what had already happened to me through the Holy Spirit. I spent my junior and high school years at this church.

Shortly after graduating from high school, we moved to California. Soon after, I volunteered for the draft and was sent to Alaska with the U.S. Army. It was there that I met Gwen, my wife. My relationship with the Lord became very tender and personal. When I learned how to study the scriptures, I began absorbing God's love and learned of His purpose in my life. I had always acquired knowledge about Jesus from other people. The difference today is that I now own that knowledge and it has become my own through personal study of the scriptures and teachings by the Holy Spirit.

Ervin L. Steele

Jesus Is Coming—A Different Perspective